TABLE OF
CONTENTS

INTRODUCTION

READ TOGETHER AS A GROUP
WHEN BOOKS ARE HANDED OUT

Our Mission

Hebrews 10:12-13 *But when this priest had offered for all time one sacrifice for sins, he sat down at the right hand of God, and since that time he waits for his enemies to be made his footstool.*
Also see: **Acts 2:34, Psalm 110, Matt 22:44**

The Lord is waiting. He is waiting for His Kings and Priests to rule and reign over His enemy with Him. He is waiting to return with the fullness of His Kingdom until we have completed our assignment on earth, a land of opposition. Although the enemy will be thrown into the lake of fire (**Rev 20:10**) and will not exist in heaven, we were made to be free and the Lord wants to be with a people that uses their freedom to choose Him. He wants to be with co-heirs that conquered through His Spirit, so no other opponent will again arise in His perfect government. Together we will learn how God's Kingdom is not like the kingdoms of this earth. On this earth, He conquered by loving not His life unto death. As His ambassadors, we are called to do the same. Let's dive headlong into how we will go from glory to glory until we usher in the return of our King in the fullness of His Kingdom.

Introduction

If America was conquered by a larger, more powerful Kingdom, we would quickly understand how the concept of Kingdom works. It is reflected at every level of the empire. In conquests of days past Kings would set up their image at the boundaries of each city so the citizens would know who was king, what he looked like. This was a reminder of who was in command. In a conquest scenario, the cities, counties, states, currently operating under the laws and guidance of the American system, would come under new governance. At every level, the laws of the new governance would apply, and our current system would transform to look like the larger, more powerful Kingdom now in control, ultimately looking like the King himself. This, however, would only happen to the extent the new laws and ordinances were applied and enforced by conquerors/ambassadors of the conquering Kingdom and to the extent those ambassadors resembled the King and his rule.

In the beginning, God created the heavens and the earth. Genesis 1 then says He made man in His image. As His image bearers, if His Spirit resides in us, we are His ambassadors. If we resemble the King and administer and enforce His Kingdoms ways, this earth will be transformed to look like Him. From the largest (Heaven and all it encompasses,) to the smallest participants in God's Kingdom (our individual vessels,) this alignment first starts within. If we allow Christ's transformational work in our Spirit, soul and body, our very thinking and vision changes to manifest Kingdom around us. As we transform, God's Kingdom will be advanced in our closest surroundings first (family.) As unity and transformation happens in our homes, our churches and communities will be transformed as we bring His ways to our larger gatherings. As Christ unites us and His Holy Spirit orchestrates this work in concert across geographies, individual Kingdom functioning parts influence the whole and nations will begin to reflect the larger Kingdom of Heaven under God.

GROUP QUESTION:

- WHAT ARE YOUR CURRENT PARADIGMS THAT STAND IN THE WAY OF BELIEVING THIS IS POSSIBLE?

_____

_____

_____

In this series, we will start with the big picture of God's Kingdom. From there we will deconstruct the Kingdom into smaller and smaller parts until we get to our own individual vessels and their transformation as the Kingdom is formed inside each of us. From there we will build back up to how we, collectively as Christ's body, can stand united in our rightful position as Kings and Priests in the Kingdom of Heaven under the rule of our God right here on the earth. As we progress through this study together, we will see how Jesus' entrance and victory over the earthly Kingdom actually ushered in the laws and ordinances of a larger, more powerful, never-ending Kingdom. Together we will take steps of learning how to get beyond our "flesh blindfolds" and operate in His Kingdom, one without beginning or end. We will learn the story of our King, His Kingdom and our part in it.

Prayer

Holy Spirit, give me eyes to see and ears to hear You. Please remove all preconceived thoughts and ideas I bring here today. You say my eyes are the windows to my soul, and I confess my soul has been corrupted by what I have seen and limited by what I have understood. God, you know ALL. I ask you to transform me today, throughout this study and throughout my life until I look like You.

The goal of this prayer is to reset the distorted worldviews we each bring. Our lens has been dirtied by our limited experiences (and this is the case even for the most experienced among the group.) We are submitting to God who wants to give us His view and heavenly perspective.

GROUP DISCUSSION

WHAT DO YOU FEEL LIKE THE LORD IS CALLING YOU TO IN THIS SEASON? WHAT ARE YOUR FEELINGS ABOUT GOING "ALL IN" TO A PLACE OF FULL SURRENDER TO THE LORD?

GROUP ACTIVITY

WHAT IS YOUR TESTIMONY (HISTORY WITH THE LORD?)

THE KINGDOM OF GOD

What was God's purpose in creating us? Do our lives reflect His purpose and intention, made possible by His sacrifice, or are we living in much smaller stories? In the next 12 weeks, we will go on a journey through time to partner with God in stepping into our roles as Kingdom ambassadors with Him as our King.

Does something inside you quiver at the thought of being a conqueror (a Kingdom ambassador?) Perhaps that is driven by the misuse of power you have witnessed in the past, your own feelings of insecurity and self-doubt or doctrines you have believed? Let's explore Genesis to Revelation and Jesus' triumphant entry to gain both focus and broaden our view of the story you are in.

In the beginning, God created the heavens and the earth... Then God said, "Let us make mankind in our image, in our likeness, so that they may rule over the fish in the sea and the birds in the sky, over the livestock and all the wild animals, and over all the creatures that move along the ground. So God created mankind in his own image, in the image of God he created them; male and female he created them. God blessed them and said to them, "Be fruitful and increase in number; fill the earth and subdue it. Rule over the fish in the sea and the birds in the sky and over every living creature that moves on the ground." **Genesis 1:1, 1:26-28 NIV**

In verse 28 the Hebrew this word for dominion is radah. It's a royal word associated with kingship. Unfortunately, we lost our ability to take dominion over the earth after the fall in Genesis 3, instead being deceived to set up kingdoms in our own image. However, at that time God foretold a time when lasting victory would come from the seed of the woman, and 4,000 years later He Himself arrived on the scene. Since we could no longer be like God after the fall, God's plan was to become like us so we could once again be like Him, carry His image and be true ambassadors of His Kingdom.

Before His arrival as Jesus, however, the Old Testament records the journey to the fulfillment of this beautiful promise. Like with every great story, this one is rich with foreshadowing. A wonderful illustration is in the name of the family God would later come into, this is none other than Israel, literally in Hebrew "Triumphant with God", "who prevails with God." The name of the family literally means conquering with God!

READ GENESIS 35:9-12

QUESTION:

- WHAT WAS THE FIRST THING GOD TOLD JACOB TO DO AFTER HE CHANGED HIS NAME?

_____

_____

_____

_____

_____

Once again, just like in the very beginning, God is blessing a man, giving him a new name and instructing him to be fruitful and multiply. At the time of this promise, the man did not yet have the authority to take dominion and bear God's image fully, however, Jesus was to soon enter the scene to make it possible.

In more glorious foreshadowing, before His own entrance into the world through the family bearing the name of His plans, we again see the word "radah." This time it is used right in the middle of human history (in approximately 1,000 BC, 3,000 years after Adam and 3,000 years from the present) and right in the middle of the Bible in Psalm 72. It is originally a coronation Psalm for Solomon, King of Israel at the height of its empire but also speaks to a future time of fulfillment of the Kingdom under King Jesus.

May he defend the afflicted among the people and save the children of the needy; may he crush the oppressor... May he rule from sea to sea and from the River to the ends of the earth... For he will deliver the needy who cry out, the afflicted who have no one to help. He will take pity on the weak and the needy and save the needy from death. He will rescue them from oppression and violence, for precious is their blood in his sight. **Psalm 72:4, 8, 12-14 NIV**

QUESTION:
- WHAT DOES RULING LOOK LIKE IN GOD'S EYES?

_____

_____

_____

_____

_____

_____

_____

_____

May he have dominion [*radah*] from sea to sea . . . Verses 4 and 12-14 then display what that dominion, that radah, looks like: to bring redemption to the poor, to literally help heal the brokenhearted, to crush the oppressor.

The conquering that God desires is given further clarification as a type that protects the defenseless and provides justice to the oppressed. To exercise dominion over creation therefore means to honor and protect it. So going back to the beginning, a paraphrase of our original instructions from God in **Genesis 1:28** expanding on radah might read: *"Be fruitful and have children, caring for My creation by filling the earth and conquering everything in it that leads to death. I am giving you the ultimate challenge to be an ambassador of my ways over the natural world, over the diversity of all My beautiful creatures."*

Like Jacob when he received his new name, Solomon and Israel did not yet have the authority and therefore the ability to have lasting dominion. So, after falling back into idolatry and unbelief under kings that set up kingdoms in their own images and images of this world, Israel was conquered and only a small remnant of the people returned to and populated the land by the time of Jesus' arrival. The Law became religion and approximately 1,000 years after Solomon we find Israel under subjection to the Roman kingdom. This is the backdrop for the Lord's fulfillment of His promise.

"The Spirit of the Lord is on me, because he has anointed me to proclaim good news to the poor. He has sent me to proclaim freedom for the prisoners and recovery of sight for the blind, to set the oppressed free." **Luke 4:18-19 NIV**

QUESTION:
- WHAT SIMILARITIES EXIST BETWEEN THE PASSAGE IN PSALM 72 AND THIS ONE?

_____

_____

_____

_____

After waiting until the age of 30 upon completion of the 40 day temptation in the wilderness, the Lord announced His royal entrance in the temple by reading the Words He gave the prophet Isaiah 700 years before. The Words described the type and nature of His rule. This announcement was the earthly fulfillment of the promise to Adam and Eve and in complete alignment with His concept of radah shared through the King and prophet David for his son Solomon in Psalm 72 after commencing his 40 year reign. The religious leaders celebrated the memories of David and Solomon, but their lens for kingdom was polluted by man's form of reign, most recently evidenced by how they were being ruled over by the Romans. They lost God's concept of radah and tried to immediately kill Jesus by throwing Him off a cliff right after this announcement. Two kingdom's were clashing, one would later prevail at the cross.

The Greek word for Kingdom is Basileia, which means royal power, kingship, dominion, rule. The gospel writers use the term 120 times. By contrast, the phrase "born again," is used only once. When you read the gospels with this in mind, you will find that nearly every parable Jesus told was about the Kingdom. Jesus announced God's way of doing business, and He would have but a short time to train His co-heirs on how His Kingdom functions. With each parable, every teaching moment, interaction and miracle, He plays the role of chief architect, illustrating the blueprints to His builders in 4D. The Words are recorded (ultimately becoming the Bible,) and like blueprints, provide a detailed plan for the builders to follow. That stated, if you've ever built before, particularly something that's never been built, you know how many questions you have when you read the plans! So Jesus promised and provided His Holy Spirit as foreman to ensure all the different pieces come together as planned. With the plans and provision set in place, the Lord gives His final instructions.

And Jesus came up and spoke to them, saying, "All authority has been given to Me in heaven and on earth. "Go therefore and make disciples of all the nations, baptizing them in the name of the Father and the Son and the Holy Spirit, teaching them to observe all that I commanded you; and lo, I am with you always, even to the end of the age." **Matthew 28:18-20 NIV**

QUESTION:

• WHAT IS THE CONNECTION BETWEEN GOD'S FIRST WORDS TO ADAM IN GENESIS 1:26 AND JESUS' FINAL INSTRUCTIONS BEFORE ASCENDING BACK INTO HEAVEN?

_____

_____

_____

_____

_____

_____

_____

_____

_____

_____

_____

_____

_____

_____

Before He ascended back into heaven, in the presence of His ambassadors, the Lord tells them how radah will be accomplished. A paraphrase: "Go make disciples of the entire earth, baptize them and teach them to do everything you saw Me do." It's the same mandate from God to Adam and Eve in Genesis 1, but now with explicit instructions on how to do it! It was now time. All they needed was His power. Ten days later, Acts 2 records the outpouring of the Spirit on these same ambassadors.

Years have passed. Almost 2,000 of them. Each one demonstrating the patience of the Lord with us to accomplish the task He assigned with His first Words to mankind in Genesis and final Words before ascending. The amount of time required has not been a surprise to Him, so He went ahead and gave us the book of Revelation to confirm His plans. To tell of what's ahead and cement the victory with tomorrow's headlines today. Does the book of Revelation mention the same radah theme?

The answer is a resounding yes! In fact, it provides probably the most dramatic evidence that God's plans never changed from Genesis 1 (4,000 BC,) Psalm 72 (1,000 BC,) Isaiah 61 (700 BC,) Jesus' ministry (30 AD) to the prophecies found in Revelation (70AD – now.)

The book of Revelation starts off with letters to each of the 7 churches. Each of the letters ends with a promise "to him who overcomes." The word here being translated as overcomes is the Greek word Nikao (to conquer, prevail, to carry off the victory, come off victorious, of Christ, victorious over all His foes.) Are you kidding me? This is simply too good! It's radah! Let's see what these promises are for the conquerors in each of these churches:

1. "I will give to eat from the tree of life, which is in the midst of the Paradise of God."
2. "shall not be hurt by the second death."
3. "I will give some of the hidden manna to eat."
4. I will give him a white stone, and on the stone a new name written which no one knows except him who receives it.'"
5. "to him I will give power over the nations."
6. "shall be clothed in white garments."
7. "I will not blot out his name from the Book of Life."
8. "I will confess his name before My Father and before His angels."

9. "I will make him a pillar in the temple of My God, and he shall go out no more."
10. "I will write on him the name of My God and the name of the city of My God, the New Jerusalem, which comes down out of heaven from My God."
11. "I will write on him My new name."
12. "I will grant to sit with Me on My throne, as I also overcame (conquered) and sat down with My Father on His throne."

Are you ready to be tortured, ridiculed, made to look like a fool, surrender your life and go all in after reading these promises? Words can't describe what is in store for us! We must get a picture of what this looks like and hold fast to it. This is the story of our family. Paul states that he who is really of Israel is one who is inwardly, by the Spirit of God. The word translated as "gentiles" is ethnos, which really means nations. When you believe, surrender your life to Jesus and receive His Spirit you become part of the family. So God is literally making all the nations into one family, created to conquer the earth with Him. Need more evidence? Paul goes on to call us "more than conquerors," "co-heirs with Christ," and even says "don't you know you will judge angels." Peter calls us a "chosen people, a royal priesthood, a holy nation." **Rev 5:10** the Spirit confesses *"You have made them to be a kingdom and priests to serve our God, and they will reign on the earth."*

Ready to conquer but old doctrines holding you back? Don't let them! We won't spend long on this, but many popular Christian doctrines hold to a theology of defeat, as if the enemy rules every "mountain of society" until Christ plucks us up to save us. Sound familiar? What is the fruit produced by holding to this doctrine? Fear, which yields us to inactivity! It is far from what the early church believed, and is a recent doctrine, showing up only in the last few centuries and popularized by editor's notes placed in the widely-circulated Scofield Bible. Yes, there will be persecution in the end, but that's because we're doing our part. The enemy's final desperate moves are from a defensive position, not because he has all but won! Pin an opponent in a corner and you get a desperate response!

It is written. This will happen. However, the Kingdom must first be formed within us, our families and churches before we will see our communities and the world ultimately changed to reflect His perfect ways

QUESTION:
· WHAT IS THE HOLY SPIRIT SAYING TO ME?

_____

_____

_____

_____

_____

_____

_____

_____

_____

_____

_____

_____

_____

_____

GROUP DISCUSSION:

- HOW DO YOU FEEL ABOUT BEING A CONQUEROR? WHAT MIGHT HOLD YOU BACK?
- WHAT ARE SOME OTHER DOCTRINES YOU HOLD ONTO THAT MAY GET IN THE WAY? WHAT COULD BE THE FRUIT IN YOUR LIFE IF YOU TRULY BELIEVED THIS IS GOD'S PLAN FOR YOUR LIFE?

_____

_____

_____

_____

_____

_____

_____

_____

_____

_____

_____

_____

_____

GROUP ACTIVITY:
- BREAK INTO GROUPS OF 3 AND PRAY BLESSINGS OVER EACH OTHER.
- LET THE HOLY SPIRIT GUIDE THE WORDS AND LISTEN FOR ANYTHING ELSE HE MAY WANT YOU TO PRAY ABOUT TOGETHER.

THE CHURCH

03

This week we will be looking at foundations and history of the church and its role in the Kingdom of God. Let's start by looking at the word from which we get the word church, "ecclesia". This Greek word appears in the New Testament approximately 115 times. The Greek word "ecclesia" is defined as: "The called-out (ones)" [ECC = out; KALEO = call]. Thus, you can see how this word was used to indicate a body of selected people.

Quoting from the Oxford Universal English Dictionary on the word "ecclesia": Ecclesia [mediaeval Latin, and Greek - from: SUMMONED]-A regularly convoked assembly, especially the general assembly of Athenians. Later, the regular word for church.

An "ecclesia" was originally a select civil body, summoned or convoked for a particular purpose. What, then, did the writers of the New Testament mean when they used the word "ecclesia" to describe a Christian body of people? It's reasonable to assume they were speaking of a body of Christians called out of the Roman and Judean systems to gather as a family/community under King Jesus. And that was the reason these same Christians ran into trouble with kings and rulers; were arrested, crucified and martyred. Let's look at the earliest gatherings of called out ones, formed right at the fountainhead of the first outpouring of the Holy Spirit in Acts and functioning as one under His guidance.

READ: ACTS 2:42-47 AND ACTS 4:29-35

QUESTION:
• WHAT STANDS OUT TO YOU MOST ABOUT THIS FIRST CHURCH?

_____

_____

_____

_____

_____

_____

This is the purest form of Christ's body operating together in unity only found in God's Kingdom. It is hardly more than a mustard seed in a big garden in the context of the global population at this point, but it's unlike anything the earth had seen. Genuine freedom, signs and wonders performed by regular people, people forsaking their personal riches to help others. The growth doesn't come from programs and evangelism techniques, rather it says "the Lord added to their number daily." It's a group of people so in love with their King and amazed at His power others can't help but show up and get saved. They were all in, willing to do everything the King instructed. The Holy Spirit's presence created an environment so intoxicating they ALL sold everything they had. Regardless of your political stance, you have to agree this was special. Let's review the checklist of what they allowed the Holy Spirit to do among them, causing their church to be a catalyst for the global growth of Christianity:

1.   Devoted themselves to the Apostles teaching
2.   Devoted themselves to fellowship
3.   Devoted themselves to prayer
4.   Devoted themselves to eating together
5.   Filled with awe at the signs and wonders performed by the Apostles
6.   Praised God together
7.   Enjoyed the favor of all the people
8.   Went to temple (church) together
9.   The Lord added to their number daily

That sounds pretty awesome. Let me assure you the Lord desires this for His people. He is both willing and able to pour this out on His body at any time. What happened to this church and why doesn't it look quite like this today? In short, satan has waged his retaliation on several fronts, but perhaps none more deceiving than his efforts to short circuit unity in Christ's body through the introduction of division and mixture. Jesus said "A house divided against itself cannot stand" and His enemy has implemented the tactic. Let's look at the first "mixture" that came in and the punishment levied for the tarnishing of the pure thing Jesus was enjoying and blessing so richly:

READ: ACTS 5:1-11

QUESTION:
   • WHY DO YOU THINK THE PUNISHMENT FOR ANANIAS AND SAPHIRA WAS SO SEVERE?

_____

_____

_____

_____

_____

The honeymoon period of the church didn't appear to last long. It is difficult to find a modern equivalent to what happened to Ananias and Saphira. Can you imagine the fear of dropping dead for an 8% tithe? Even in the age of grace, Ananias and Saphira bore the punishment for what they were ushering into the united assembly. They were the first to introduce division and mixture from satan that would aim to dilute Christ's body for the next 2,000 years.
Paul's numerous writings to the churches in Corinth, Ephesus, Galatia and beyond provided warnings about others bringing this mixture into other newly formed ecclesias. He frequently admonished them to return to their first love. Jude does the same and this warning is the focus of his brief letter:

Beloved, while I was making every effort to write you about our common salvation, I felt the necessity to write to you appealing that you contend earnestly for the faith which was once for all handed down to the saints. For certain persons have crept in unnoticed, those who were long beforehand marked out for this condemnation, ungodly persons who turn the grace of our God into licentiousness and deny our only Master and Lord, Jesus Christ. **Jude 1:3-4, NIV**

QUESTION:
- WHAT DO THESE PEOPLE WHO HAVE WORMED IN DO?
- WHY ARE THEY SO DANGEROUS?

_____

_____

_____

_____

_____

Jesus says you will know them by their fruit. Bad fruit divides. Could we possibly ignore the changes that have taken place from the original fountainhead of the Spirit until this present moment? Our King and Savior was patient in His sufferings and dealings with us during His ministry, but my goodness has He been patient while waiting for us to return to our original position as united members of His own body!

We see this as His heart's cry during the final moments before He was taken into custody. In fact, it is the crescendo of Jesus' longest unbroken monologue from John 14-17, four chapters of Jesus pouring out His heart until His ultimate prayer and expressed desire occurs in 17.

READ JOHN 17:9-11 AND 18-23

The patience of Jesus! He is desperate for our unity, for our Oneness with Him and each other. We are the called-out ones of the world!

The ecclesia is the gathering of the called-out ones...it happens any time we assemble. Jesus and His Spirit is the head, the teacher when we gather and as His body we each participate in unity. This can only happen in an environment of oneness designed above. What is designed above is opposed on earth. So naturally, opposition springs up as God moves. It has happened during every known revival and occurred throughout the Gospels and New Testament. It was also prophesied to happen inside the body of believers in the end times. It is indeed the clash of two kingdoms. Paul wrote to Timothy as a warning.

But realize this, that in the last days difficult times will come. For men will be lovers of self, lovers of money, boastful, arrogant, revilers, disobedient to parents, ungrateful, unholy, unloving, irreconcilable, malicious gossips, without self-control, brutal, haters of good, treacherous, reckless, conceited, lovers of pleasure rather than lovers of God, holding to a form of godliness, although they have denied its power; Avoid such men as these. **2 Timothy 3:1-5 NIV**

"Having the appearance of godliness, but denying its power." Ouch! These are definitely religious folks he is talking about. Probably people that appear to be doing a good job at checking the boxes...sowing discord is made easier when you look the part. This isn't to say they are the enemy. The enemy is the enemy, these people are just unwittingly partnering with his plans. We know Paul isn't talking about the world, because in 1 Cor 5:9-11 he speaks to exactly this. He knows the world is already like this, but he is talking about the church.

Let's not be discouraged. This is all warning and pretext to what God is actually doing on the earth right now in our generation. It is amidst this backdrop that a genuine reformation back to the original fountainhead of the Spirit is forming. We must earnestly seek unity in His Spirit and the purest, simplest form of gathering together as a family of called-out ones. In order to do so, we each need a personal revival in the Spirit (next chapters) in our generation. Interestingly, one meaning of the word generation is the word "circle." As Jesus takes us back to our beginning by making us a united body once again (in even greater fullness) to complete a 2,000+ year circle, let's see if the Word had a summary of what we've just experienced as a body.

READ REV 12:12-17

QUESTION:
   • HOW DO YOU FEEL SATAN HAS MADE WAR AGAINST YOU?

_____

_____

_____

_____

_____

"He went to make war on the rest of her offspring." How does the devil go about warfare? We know he masquerades as an angel of light **2 Corinthians 11:14**, so perhaps his strategy was indeed "mixing in?" Let's review what happened after our original united church and Paul's letters (mostly warnings) were sent to the other early churches. In Rev 18:4 the Lord implores us to "Come out of her my people." We are His people and we are in something He wants us to come out of. The context of this passage is Babylon. Babylon has a long history, but is the place where men built a tower to reach the heavens and a place where religion sprang from during Israel's captivity. It is important to know what we are coming out of, so here is a brief review of institutional church history:

The church grew amidst a backdrop of mixture, opposition and the martyrdom of the faithful as higher criticism and reasoning came into the faith. By 250 A.D widespread violent universal persecution of Christianity by the Romans intensified. The reason for the persecutions was mainly that the Roman Empire was beginning to crumble and the emperor was calling for absolute submission to his authority. Christians could not give them this submission because Jesus was King and they owed their allegiance to Him. In 312 A.D Constantine accepted Christianity as an official Roman Religion after seeing a vision of the cross and hearing the words "Go forth and conquer" and a critical moment came in the establishment of the church as an "institution" came when Emperor Constantine made Christianity mainstream in 381, naming it as Rome's official religion. Unfortunately, the Roman form of conquering did not follow God's Psalm 72, Isaiah 61 and Matthew 28 plans. The adoption of Christianity did initially end much of the persecution of that era, but invited even more mixture into the stream of the original outpouring of the Spirit in Acts.

As the institutional church and as it's hierarchy grew in stature, persecutions of the true disciples of Jesus began to concurrently grow. What is considered the "Dark Ages" ensued, with an estimated 1,000 years of pain and torment for those who were loyal to the True King's domain (Kingdom – "kings domain.") Printed Bibles in any form were scarce and rarely found in a language other than Latin. The power struggle was so great, that one historian records:
This was a time, when not only was the Bible banned, but literacy in general was prohibited and frowned upon. Very few people during this time knew how to read or write. The Institutional Church was determined that the less knowledge that people had, the easier it would be to rule them. "Only ten percent of people in the Roman Empire could read...and those were generally in the wealthy upper classes." -River of God, Gregory J. Riley, pp. 66
The Institutional Church admits this in her own Law on several occasions during this period, one such example is found in The Council of Tarragona of 1234, in its second canon, ruled that:
"No one may possess the books of the Old and New Testaments, and if anyone possesses them he must turn them over to the local bishop within eight days, so that they may be burned..."– **The Church Council of Tarragona 1234 AD; 2nd Cannon – Source : D. Lortsch, Historie de la Bible en France, 1910, p.14.**

QUESTION:

• HOW WOULD YOUR FAITH BE IF YOU DIDN'T KNOW ANYONE WITH A BIBLE?

_____

_____

_____

_____

The consequences of misalignment with the doctrines of the Institutional church were grave. Another historian records that:
"...it is estimated by careful and credible historians, that more than fifty millions of the human family, have been slaughtered for the crime of heresy by persecutors within the church, an average of more than forty thousand religious murders for every year..."- **History of Romanism," pp. 541, 542. New York: 1871**.

In 1517 things began to turn with the publishing of Martin Luther's Ninety-Five thesis and the emergence of the Protestant reformation, deriving its name from those who openly protested the practices of the institutional church. Remembering that history is His Story, the Lord saw fit to have the printing press and widespread translation of the Word into the languages of the people coincide with this reformation, bringing about the first seismic shift in the ecclesia in a millennia. The enlightenment church, modern church and post-modern churches have followed along with outpourings of the Spirit, revivals and pseudo-reformations. Every major move of God has been described as "messy," but the Kingdom is no doubt accelerating at a pace not seen since the original outpouring. It is now believed that more have come to Christ since the Azusa Street outpouring of the Spirit in the 110 years since 1906 than in the 1900 years combined that came before! All of creation is indeed anxiously awaiting the Sons of God to be revealed (Rom 8:19,) and this is happening!

The acceleration is no doubt of people coming in the doors to the Kingdom, but there is much opportunity for them to step into their roles and destinies as conquerors, no longer being conformed to the patterns of this world:

- Roughly same # of marriages in church and secular culture end in divorce.
- Research shows the rates for drug, alcohol and pornography addictions are the same inside and outside the church.
- Only 15% of the 360k churches in the U.S. are growing.
- Only 2-5% of the growing churches are growing by new conversions to Christ.
- 90% of evangelical church members do not share their faith.
- 50% of all evangelical churches did not have a single convert last year.
- Only 51% of pastors & 19% of confessed born-again believers have

what is defined as a Biblical world view (absolute moral truths exist, the Bible is totally accurate in all principles it teaches, satan is considered to be a real being or force and not merely symbolic, a person cannot earn their way into heaven, Jesus lived a sin free life on earth, God is the all-knowing, all-powerful creator of the world who still rules the universe today.)

- 70% of people raised in the church leave it between the ages of 18-23.
- Christians on average give 2-3% of their income.
  Source: Barna Research Group, 2008-2016

Our King has given us the edict to be salt and light to this world. There is a culture of heaven that wants to break through to the earth, but the statistics show the mixture Paul warned us about has mixed in thoroughly. We have too often been conformed to the pattern of this world rather than allowing the Lord to transform us. Our King's famous sermon on the mount tells us that in the Kingdom, change first starts within each of us. Before change comes to the church, the Kingdom must first be formed within each of us and within our homes. Next week we will look at how that happens.

GROUP DISCUSSION:
- WHY IS IT IMPORTANT TO GATHER IN SMALL SIZE GROUPS?
- WHAT IS GOD'S PURPOSE IN THESE GATHERINGS?
- WHAT FEELINGS DID YOU WORK THROUGH AS YOU READ ABOUT THE HISTORY OF THE CHURCH THIS WEEK?

GROUP ACTIVITY:
- DIVIDE INTO GROUPS OF 4 AND SHARE YOUR PERSONAL CHURCH
- HISTORY WITH ONE ANOTHER (INCLUDE SMALL GROUP HISTORY SHARING STORIES.)

THE KINGDOM WITHIN

04

In 1 Corinthians 3:16 Paul writes: "Do you not know that you yourselves are God's temple, and that God's Spirit dwells in you?" He goes on to state it again in chapter 6. The concept was founded way back in Genesis when God breathed His Spirit Life into Adam at our very conception, animating his body. When Solomon completed the first temple in 2 Chronicles 7 then "...the Glory of the Lord filled the temple." This means it was only a really, really nice building before God's presence came into it. Adam probably had a very impressive looking body, but it was lifeless before God breathed into it. The revelation here is that we are vessels, containers designed to be filled with God's own Spirit.

READ: JOHN 2:12-22

This passage is fascinating for a number of reasons, but a deeper question surfaces. Was Jesus zealous for the building and its courtyards? If the structures, why did He allow them to be completely destroyed in 70 A.D.? God's valued currency here (and everywhere else in scripture) is clearly His people. When you invite Jesus into your heart He becomes a temple raider, whipping out every enemy to the very extent we will allow Him to. He is a jealous God and He wants our vessels filled with Him, and that's what is best for us!

"When the unclean spirit goes out of a man, it passes through waterless places seeking rest, and not finding any, it says, 'I will return to my house from which I came.' "And when it comes, it finds it swept and put in order. "Then it goes and takes along seven other spirits more evil than itself, and they go in and live there; and the last state of that man becomes worse than the first." **Luke 11:24-26 NIV**

QUESTION:
- IS IT ENOUGH TO BE EMPTIED OF THE SPIRITS OF THIS WORLD, OR DO WE
- NEED TO BE FILLED TO THE BRIM SO THERE IS NO ROOM LEFT IN OUR HOUSE? WHY?

_____

_____

_____

_____

_____

God's Spirit lives in you, however, you are now a child of the Light. Just like in life, in God's Kingdom there is a way things work. God has established the rules and boundaries and we have an enemy that, although forced to operate within them, impersonates God with the exact opposite agenda. Our house/temple is designed to be filled. Here we see a clean house that doesn't get filled with the Spirit of God, so he is a ripe target to get filled nonetheless. There are only two kingdoms. The kingdom of darkness and the Kingdom of our God in heaven. If you are like me, you have spent countless hours unknowingly programming yourself to be in sync with the kingdom of this world, which is the kingdom of darkness. Now that God's Spirit lives in us, we are children of the Light. This fact is the central dynamic of the New Testament and how the apostles and early believers lived the supernatural lives they did.

"for where your treasure is, there your heart will be also. "The eye is the lamp of the body; so then if your eye is clear, your whole body will be full of light. "But if your eye is bad, your whole body will be full of darkness. If then the light that is in you is darkness, how great is the darkness! **Matthew 6:21-23 NIV**

The eye is a lens. Through it we see the world. Clear vision here would be to see like Jesus and see..._"what I see the Father doing."_ This is available to us when we walk in the Spirit. Most of us, however, accept Christ and even receive

His Spirit, but still feel stuck. Perhaps our lens is dirty? Perhaps we've had a foul power at work, entering our eye gates and ear gates for countless hours from our youth? Ephesians 2:2 says this was our story: *in which you once walked, following the course of this world, following the prince of the power of the air, the spirit that is now at work in the sons of disobedience.* At no time in history has the kingdom of darkness had a tool that can transform the human mind like it does in our era with media.

QUESTION:

- WHAT ARE SOME WAYS YOUR LENS (WORLDVIEW) HAS BEEN DIRTIED BY THE WORLD, OR EVEN RELIGION?

_____

_____

_____

_____

Do not conform to the pattern of this world, but be transformed by the renewing of your mind. Then you will be able to test and approve what God's will is--his good, pleasing and perfect will. **Romans 12:2 NIV**

A few years ago IBM announced their predictions for computing's future, stating that within 5 years all 5 senses will be involved. In their own words: Touch: You will be able to touch through your phone, Sight: A pixel will be worth a thousand words, Hearing: Computers will hear what matters, Taste: Digital taste buds will help you to eat smarter, Smell: Computers will have a sense of smell. With more and more of our human senses being involved, our decisions about our own participation and involvement are more critical than ever, as we run the risk of being swept away into the world's current without even realizing it. No doubt, the enemy's plans are to mitigate Christianity to a mere cultural or mental ascent while we are unwitting to the fact of his ownership of our very own mindspace. There is only one solution: we need to be completely renewed by His Holy Spirit within us. One big drag, especially for American Christians, is that renewal takes time and effort. I believe that's why Paul preceded Romans 12:2 with Romans 12:1 *"Therefore I urge you, brothers, on account of God's mercy, to offer your bodies as living sacrifices, holy and pleasing to God, which is your spiritual service of worship."* Let's face it, the temple was a place for sacrifices. Just because our microwave culture has lost track of that doesn't make it not true. Our body is a living sacrifice. Can we get serious about the transformation process and fill our eye and ear gates with His Voice, worship and His Word? We've had 20, 30, 40+ years or more being bombarded by what amounts to the devil's messaging and airwaves, do I offend you by suggesting we may need more than 15 minutes a day with the Lord to renew our thinking? As you read His Word through a sanctified lens (that we completely right with God in Christ,) I promise your hunger for it will increase and it won't feel like duty. But how can we be set free from trying to "earn" our way to Him?

But if you bite and devour one another, take care that you are not consumed by one another. But I say, walk by the Spirit, and you will not carry out the desire of the flesh. For the flesh sets its desire against the Spirit, and the Spirit against the flesh; for these are in opposition to one another, so that you may not do the things that you please. **Galatians 5:15-17 NIV**

The Spirit is a consuming fire, sent to purify our temples so God can reside in a holy environment, ready for good works.

"I baptize you with water...He will baptize you with the Holy Spirit and fire." **Luke 3:16 NIV**

If the Spirit dwells within us, walking by the Spirit is our key to change. But how do we walk by the Spirit? Is this being modeled well by anyone you know? It can seem abstract without an example to see and follow. Trying our best, let's run through a hypothetical situation. Let's say you're barely making your bills each month, you stop at a gas station while running late for work and someone opens your passenger door and steals your cell phone while you're pumping gas. Based on your background and experiences there are a myriad of reactions you can have in a moment like this. Fear, panic, rage, etc. You could run in and call the police, try to chase the perpetrator down in your car, sit down and cry, start drinking, on and on we go. As a growing Christian you opt against one of the "worse" reactions and choose fear. You sit in your car and worry your butt off about not being able to afford another phone, losing your job, boyfriend, car and as worry goes things get out of hand and escalate. You make it to work and your friend from church reminds you that Jesus said not to worry, so you decide to try. As you do, you end up focusing on your circumstances even more and things only get worse! You've spent so many years of your life handling problems this way that incorporating Jesus' teachings are great in theory, but not of much practical value in the moment.

Does this process sound familiar?
Perhaps it's the betrayal of a friend, loss of a job, financial/relational strain, the list goes on and on of our daily challenges on this earth. The question is are we living by principals (religion and tree of knowledge of good and evil) or are we allowing His Spirit to transform us in each of these situations? The renewal work we've done in the Word will help us immensely when we encounter daily troubles because we will have the Word welling up inside when trouble arises.

Even so, we need a default process of tuning in to the Spirit within during these moments (and all the non-crisis moments throughout our day) to start walking in the Spirit regularly. Good news! This is exactly the type of practical, naturally supernatural Christian living we will be diving into in weeks to come! It is a beautiful facet of Kingdom living.

QUESTION:
- WHAT TYPES OF THINGS SEEMS TO THROW YOU OFF CONSISTENTLY?
- WHAT WOULD IT LOOK LIKE FOR YOU TO ASK FOR THE HOLY SPIRIT'S HELP IN THOSE MOMENTS?

_____

_____

_____

_____

_____

As a brief summary, we are vessels intended to be filled with God's Spirit and Presence. Even after receiving His Spirit there is still work to be done. As newborn babes, we must learn how to walk "Spiritually." Even as we learn to walk, we must be careful not to slip into religion which creates bondage. Where the Spirit of the Lord is there is freedom. There are two ways to keep the Law, which is good and here to protect us. One is to seek to try to do it by ourselves. The other is to walk by the Spirit. God's abiding Presence and walking by the Spirit is the only thing that allows us to live the supernatural lives we were made to live. If we don't remain in this and encourage each other to do the same, we will slip back into religion.

QUESTION:
- WHAT IS THE HOLY SPIRIT SAYING TO ME?

_____

_____

_____

_____

_____

_____

_____

_____

_____

_____

GROUP DISCUSSION:
- WHAT DOES A RENEWAL PROCESS LOOK LIKE?
- WHAT WILL IT TAKE IN ORDER FOR OUR MINDS TO BE RENEWED?

Paul describes what appears to be an ongoing process of transformation. Perhaps this process is because there are two kingdoms in operation, the smaller, which our physical senses seem to be in subjection to, and the larger, which governs our spiritual senses and eternity. How can our physical minds be transformed to reflect this eternal Kingdom with unending peace? If we have spent countless hours in practices that have conformed our minds to the pattern of this world, what are some practices we can put in place to transform our minds to reflect the Kingdom of Heaven under our God?

_____

_____

_____

_____

_____

_____

GROUP ACTIVITY:
- SPLIT INTO GROUPS OF THREE AND BE OPEN AND VULNERABLE. WHAT DO YOU FEEL THE HOLY SPIRIT IS CONVICTING YOU ABOUT ADJUSTING IN YOUR LIFE?
- WHAT COMMITMENTS ARE YOU WILLING TO MAKE IN ACCORDANCE WITH HIS LEADING?
- PRAY FOR EACH OTHER, INVITING THE SPIRIT'S FIRE TO BURN UP WHATEVER IS CURRENTLY STANDING IN THE WAY OF HIS WORK IN OUR LIVES.

FAMILY

05

Let's summarize God's history with us and our history since His arrival as described in the Scriptures and history:

1. God makes man and woman in His image and breathes His Life into us to be intimate co-heirs with Him. Literally bestows His dignity and image onto us and sets us free, because only in doing so can He become known and freely chosen. *Think about it, satan was given so much dignity he actually thought he could exalt himself above the throne of God!* **Isaiah 14:13.** He blesses us with freedom and a command to be fruitful and multiply (through families.)

2. God creates a temptation and allows a tempter in the garden. Why? The Training ground for conquering must be in a backdrop of opposition, literally having something to conquer. God allows for an enemy to train God's co-heirs to one day look like Him (literally the preparing of the bride Jesus speaks of.) The role of the enemy is to one day be ruled over by these co-heirs (**Luke 10:19** *I have given you authority over all the power of the enemy, and you can walk among snakes and scorpions and crush them. Nothing will injure you. NLT)*

3. Man and woman fall to the lie and give away their ability to conquer to gain what they already possessed (to be like God.)

4. Through Abraham God chooses a family to work with and eventually come through. Their name (Israel) means "ruling with God."

5. Since man could no longer be like God due to the fall, God becomes like man so man could once again be like Him

to accomplish His plan that we would be like Him. God ushers in and demonstrates His Kingdom rule, restoring what was lost in the garden.

6. God pours out His Spirit and the early gatherings experience unprecedented unity, joy and miracles, but mixture comes in quickly.

7. Christianity becomes an institutional church, the Word becomes scarce (and even illegal,) and only a remnant hold to Jesus' teachings.

8. God raises protesters to reform the institution of Christianity, birthing many new movements. God releases the idea for the printing press and the Word is made available to people in their own languages in numerous countries.

9. Revivals led by the Spirit break out globally as missionaries begin to cover the globe. The number of Christians around the world nearly quadruples after the Azusa St outpouring in 1906. The totals go from 600 million in 1910 to more than 2.2 billion today, over 25% of which identify themselves as "Spirit led Christians."

10. Amidst this backdrop of growth, the prince and power of the air goes after families and they suffer unprecedented attack. The divorce rate climbs from only 7% in 1900 and peaks at over 50% by 1980. We, who are led by the Spirit and know how the story ends rise and unite and the Kingdom advances until it fulfills the Lord's prophecy that it reaches the ends of the earth.

It's good to step back and see that God has indeed been doing a patient work in His body. God's adversary has been about the same business. Unity is the result of God's work, division is the result of satan's. Let's now drill down a bit more to see what God is teaching us from this distant and recent history with the people right in front of us. If you don't have children yet, take this as a time to learn, meanwhile incorporating these concepts with other family members and friends.

Families are a place of perfecting. Our God is a practical God and He has chosen to work through family as a small and practical kingdom. This detail is not lost on the adversary, whom Jesus said was a liar from the beginning. God uses what's in front of us to teach and train us, satan wants to use the same to destroy us. Since we know God is focused on training us to rule and reign with Him as a family forever, we must learn how important it is to learn how to love and unite with the ones God has strategically predetermined to be in our earthly families. Let's emphasize that again: God has strategically predetermined our family members. Could this critical detail possibly be lost on Him? The spouse we wake up to every day, the children who will depend on us for a few decades (to a lifetime in some cases!) The parents we are to honor. If His goal is to train us to conquer would He simply put us with all amiable, well behaved, awesome people who are in no need of training themselves?

REFLECT.

- WHY DO YOU THINK GOD HAS "RIGGED" YOUR PARTICULAR FAMILY MEMBERS TO BE IN YOUR LIFE? WHAT DO YOU THINK HE IS TRYING TO DEVELOP IN YOU?

_____

_____

_____

_____

_____

_____

There is no doubt that family is often the source of our greatest grief in this life, but also our greatest joy, peace and acceptance. It is usually the place where we learn our most profound lessons, so it is a favorite teaching tool of our King. As a place of perfecting, it's usually the place where we are faced with the reality of our natural tendency towards very conditional love. "You do this and THEN I will…" We do this with spouses, as we parent, and as we are raised. Do something wrong and you usually get a scowl, punishment, a negative tone of voice or all three! We control and manipulate family members all day long with our subtle glances, voice inflections, background intel on one another and through any means necessary to get our desired outcome.

God help us! With our own conditional love and the conditional love of others smack dab in our face daily, we are faced with a terrific growing opportunity in light of the gospel. As we grow in Christ and His love leads, undoubtedly family can become the place where we will first experience God's Heavenly Kingdom on the earth. Like with His all-encompassing Kingdom, everything starts at the top though. Let's look at a dynamic that is only made possible by the Spirit of God.

READ EPHESIANS 5:22-33

QUESTION:
- WHAT IS THE HOLY SPIRIT SAYING TO YOU AS YOU READ THIS PASSAGE?
- HOW ABOUT THE ENEMY?

_____

_____

_____

_____

Is there a more debated (and avoided) passage in our modern context? Jesus tells his listeners they must eat His flesh and that offends the people of His time, but this one is multiples more offensive in our current world. How did we get so off course? Perhaps the Holy Spirit's plan would have never required the women's liberation movement? The desire of a woman's true heart is to be loved and cherished the way Jesus loves and cherishes His own body. This is not only possible, but it is His design and intention for us to discover this "mystery." That stated, it's impossible for a husband to do this for any lengthy period of time without full surrender to Jesus and His Spirit's ways. A husband must first receive love from His Father and learn how to walk in His Spirit's ways before he can love well. We must remember God's plans are good, they bring real joy, peace and real love. Indeed, if we are to experience the Kingdom in our homes it must first be an internal reality for the husband so he can love as Christ loves. This fits right into God's training for reigning plans for us. Let's look at a wife's role (and how it's equally rigged!)

READ LUKE 7:1-10

You may be wondering what this passage has to do with marriage. The Roman centurion's understanding of authority astonished Jesus. It is the only time in the gospels we see Jesus having this type of response to someone's understanding of how the Kingdom works. The passage in Ephesians requires us to have a similar understanding of Kingdom to comprehend it. Like the centurion, both husbands and wives are under authority. Our lives in Christ simply do not work unless we trust Him enough to surrender and submit our lives to His amazing and trustworthy authority. Thousands of pages could be written on this topic alone, but let's believe the Word and leave it at this: In Christ, men can love their wives and truly be that amazing and trustworthy authority that wives, in Christ, can submit to. In fulfilling the Spirit's call to unity here, we get a picture of what God's Kingdom looks like and allow heaven to manifest in our homes.

For we are God's handiwork, created in Christ Jesus to do good works, which God prepared in advance for us to do. **Ephesians 2:10 NIV**

There is another beautiful aspect of God on display in family. We get to experience, close up, a song that God is writing. The word Paul uses here is poiema, where we get our modern word poem from. Being in someone's life is to see God's story unfold in another. If you are allowing the Spirit to transform your lens (how you view the world,) you get an up-close look at a masterpiece being perfected in each of your family members! Doesn't feel like that sometimes? Then you need a bigger God! He loves each and every one of us and has even numbered the hairs on our heads (Luke 12:7,) do you think He is going to lose a single one of His own? Yes, we can get a constant fresh revelation of unconditional love through family. Through the gifts of the Spirit we each have a different expression of God, and as we grow in Him, these will be on full display in our homes.

QUESTION:
- HAVE YOU BEEN ABLE TO RECOGNIZE GOD'S HANDIWORK IN THOSE AROUND YOU?
- IF NOT CONSISTENTLY, WHAT STANDS IN THE WAY OF YOU SEEING WHAT GOD SEES IN OTHERS?

_____

_____

_____

_____

_____

_____

_____

This is not a lesson on how to fix all of your family problems. Rather, it is an encouragement to Trust a bigger God, learn how to be led by His Spirit in you and get a picture of the fruit that will be on display in your families.

Children, obey your parents in the Lord, for this is right. "Honor your father and mother"—which is the first commandment with a promise— "so that it may go well with you and that you may enjoy long life on the earth. "Fathers, do not exasperate your children; instead, bring them up in the training and instruction of the Lord. **Ephesians 6:1-4 NIV**

Continuing with the theme of authority and God's Kingdom we see the 5th commandment, which is the very first commandment for us (the first four were between us and God.) Authority structures aren't clear in our modern culture. Most media portrays children running the show to some extent. It is a subtle, but insidious attack on our very foundation of Kingdom. Children are to submit to the good authority that loves and cares for them. If they don't, our society will crumble. That is why this is the first commandment with a promise (children honor...so you will live long in the land.) Everything is undermined if the most basic unit doesn't function as God designed it to, because submission to a good authority is the way of the Kingdom. If children don't learn this in their homes, their own foundations for the Kingdom will not be put in place. What must we do? If nothing else on this earth will drive you to surrender and be led by the Spirit, it is parenting another human being. The frustrations and internal emotional swings can leave our words unchecked. These very words can bring life or death in any given moment, so if you've gone about parenting in the flesh for a while you can relate. Let me just submit to you that it's rigged by our God for our good. If we are reflective, it is also rigged so we will see the extreme grace He has shown to us (setting us free and patiently loving us through our shortcomings.) The rigging is so we learn the only way – to walk by the Spirit. Words and reactions from the Spirit bring healing. Paul instructs us not to provoke our children to anger. Parenting without the Spirit has this exact effect!

QUESTION:

- WHAT ARE SOME WAYS I HAVE EXASPERATED MY CHILDREN OR THOSE AROUND ME?
- AM I OPEN TO SLOWING DOWN ENOUGH TO HEAR WHAT THE SPIRIT IS SAYING BEFORE I REACT?

_____

_____

_____

_____

_____

_____

_____

_____

Start children off on the way they should go, and even when they are old they will not turn from it. **Proverbs 22:6 NIV**

What is the way they should go? It is the ways of our God and King. What way is that? The ways of His domain, His Kingdom. As our Father, He chose grace to mediate our differences so we could be right with Him. Perhaps we can learn from Him by walking in the Spirit in our parenting? There is no other way! We will learn more about walking in the Spirit moment by moment in Part 2 of this course, it will be essential to raising our children in the ways of the Lord.

Think about the families you really know, where you're somewhat behind the doors. I'm sure you can confirm firsthand that right now families are struggling. If we will commit to and allow for our own transformation and learn to walk in the Spirit with our families, what happened in Acts 2 will happen with us. We will be a Light to our communities and the Lord will add to our number every day. We will stand out! They will want our unity! They will ask us for advice! They will ask us for prayer! The world around us is attracted to unity because they were made for it as well!

Our churches are an extension of our families, and neither will be changed until we are transformed. The Kingdom has come, now let's allow it to be formed within us until we see it manifest all around us.

QUESTION:
    • WHAT IS THE HOLY SPIRIT SAYING TO ME?

_____

_____

_____

_____

_____

_____

GROUP DISCUSSION:

- WHY IS IT IMPORTANT FOR THE KINGDOM TO BE FORMED IN MY FAMILY?
- HOW AM I NOTICING GOD HAS SPECIFICALLY RIGGED WHO WAS TO BE IN MY LIFE? RECOGNIZING THIS RIGGING, WHERE DO I THINK HE IS LEADING ME?

_____

_____

_____

_____

_____

_____

GROUP ACTIVITY:

- BREAK INTO GROUPS OF THREE. IF LED, BE VULNERABLE ABOUT WHERE YOU HAVE STRUGGLED IN THE ROLE GOD HAS CALLED YOU TO IN YOUR FAMILY. PRAY FOR EACH OTHER, SPECIFICALLY ASKING FOR AN OPENNESS TO THE SPIRIT'S LEADING IN HELPING US WITH OUR ROLE IN OUR FAMILIES. PRAY A BLESSING OF KINGDOM UNITY ON EACH PERSONS FAMILY.

_____

_____

_____

_____

06

WORSHIP

There's an old joke about cats and dogs view of the world. A dog says "you pet me, you feed me, you shelter me, you love me. You must be God." A cat says the same exact thing but comes to a different conclusion, "you pet me, you feed me, you shelter me, you love me. I must be God." You see, the Bible is a book about God and His Kingdom, but recent generations of Western Christianity have turned it into a book about us. We go to it for solutions, for help, for guidance and it does provide all of those things, but we aren't the point. He is. Our view of the world as cats creates a grid to where our teaching, our learning, our daily activities are all generally centered on us. This "consumerism" is certainly reinforced in all media, advertising and every outlet of the kingdom of this world, but most concerning is how it has filtered into the Christian world. This approach to Christ and His Kingdom will only leave us empty, for in Him we live and move and have our being (Acts 17:28.) Since the Bible is rather a book about our King, let's go on a treasure hunt in His Word and explore where our life is actually found. He knows what we need, and as we seek and praise Him, He will provide:

Health and Blessing
Exodus 23:25 *Worship the LORD your God, and his blessing will be on your food and water. I will take away sickness from among you.*

True Comfort
2 Corinthians 1:3 *Praise be to the God and Father of our Lord Jesus Christ, the Father of compassion and the God of all comfort.*

Expansion of the Kingdom

Acts 2:46 *They broke bread in their homes and ate together with glad and sincere hearts, praising God and enjoying the favor of all the people. And the Lord added to their number daily those who were being saved.*

Real Perspective

Job 1:20-21 *At this, Job got up and tore his robe and shaved his head. Then he fell to the ground in worship and said: "Naked I came from my mother's womb, and naked I will depart. The Lord gave and the Lord has taken away; may the name of the Lord be praised."*

Answers to Questions

Acts 13:2 *While they were worshiping the Lord and fasting, the Holy Spirit said, "Set apart for me Barnabas and Saul for the work to which I have called them."*

QUESTION:

• WHY DOES GOD WANT ME TO BECOME A WORSHIPPER OF HIM?

_____

_____

_____

_____

_____

_____

_____

_____

_____

This list could go on and on. The reality is that as we praise and worship, God's provision comes into daily struggles and challenges. He created us to worship and as we do, He pours heavenly provision right back on us. Worship is the culture of heaven, so as we worship we can manifest heaven and participate in His prayer so His will can be done on earth as it is in heaven. His will is for His Kingdom to be established throughout the earth. In His Kingdom there is no longer sickness, despair, grief, pain, fear or any other thing that brings hardship into our lives.

Worship is a lifestyle of focusing on Him. It's a byproduct of everything we do in this world as we walk in the Spirit and invite Him into our jobs, families, activities and everything we do throughout the day. As we do, we experience His joy and provision for our lives. He lifts us up, and as He does, song becomes a very natural spontaneous reaction. Paul even said we can teach, admonish and get all wisdom through the songs the Spirit gives us!

Let the message of Christ dwell among you richly as you teach and admonish one another with all wisdom through psalms, hymns, and songs from the Spirit, singing to God with gratitude in your hearts. **Colossians 3:16 NIV**

How seriously did Paul take worship?

READ ACTS 16:22-34

This is extreme. Paul and Silas were so convinced about the power of worship they did it while bloodied, beaten and imprisoned with chains. Their worship caused an earthquake so strong it opened the doors and everyone's chains fell off! Do you have some chains you would still like removed? Incorporate daily worship into your life and watch them fall off. Just as our tendency is toward conditional love, our tendency is toward conditional worship. When you are walking in the Spirit that changes. Even if you're not "feeling spiritual" and the chips are down, if you've made a commitment to a lifestyle of worship you just do it, knowing God's goodness and provision is coming.

Although the fig tree shall not blossom, neither shall fruit be in the vines; the labour of the olive shall fail, and the fields shall yield no meat; the flock shall be cut off from the fold, and there shall be no herd in the stalls Yet I will rejoice in the LORD, I will joy in the God of my salvation. **Habakkuk 3:17-18 NIV**

QUESTION:
- HAS MY WORSHIP OF GOD BEEN CONDITIONAL OR UNCONDITIONAL?
- WHY?

_____

_____

_____

_____

_____

_____

You may think, "that's just not practical, I can't just spend my whole life worshipping. How am I going to pay my bills?" Don't we need to focus on our own provision? I mean, that's literally what we've been trained to do since we've entered this world! Well, in a word, you don't have to worry.

READ MATTHEW 6:25-33

Worship is seeking first His Kingdom. As you learn to focus on Jesus and tune into the flow of His Spirit throughout the day worship will flow as well. You will find the Spirit of Jesus, which is also the Spirit of Knowledge, will provide answers for those daily challenges that have been sidelining you. Where the Spirit of the Lord is there is freedom! Freedom from your struggles with your circumstances, freedom from your habits, freedom from yourself! As the saying goes, wherever you go, there you are. Usually the problem is us! So as we learn to focus on Jesus throughout our days we learn the heart of worship and become worshippers.

My mouth is filled with your praise, declaring your splendor all day long. **Psalm 71:8 NIV**

Let everything that has breath praise the Lord. Praise the Lord. **Psalm 150:6 NIV**

The book of Psalms is rich with praise of the Most High. Reading it can help turn you into a worshipper. The book ends with 6 beautiful chapters on praise and worship. Take time to read the final 6 chapters this week, allowing your heart to be fully present to each verse as you read. Turn your heart to Him and learn the art of praise. As we move into the gifts of the Holy Spirit in the weeks to follow, praise will be our path into His Presence. Psalm 100:4 Enter his gates with thanksgiving and his courts with praise; give thanks to him and praise his name.

READ: PSALM 145-150

QUESTION:
- WHAT IS THE HOLY SPIRIT SAYING TO ME?

_____

_____

_____

_____

_____

GROUP DISCUSSION:
- WHY IS WORSHIP SO IMPORTANT?
- WHAT HAVE BEEN YOUR WORSHIP PRACTICES?
- WHERE DO YOU SEE OPPORTUNITY TO WORSHIP MORE?

GROUP ACTIVITY:
- SPLIT INTO GROUPS OF FOUR. TAKE TURNS WORSHIPPING THE LORD BY EACH SHARING WHAT YOU ARE THANKFUL FOR. (TIME TO STEP OUT ON THE RISK PLANK) PRAY TOGETHER AND ASK THE SPIRIT TO LEAD YOU IN A SPONTANEOUS SONG OF THANKSGIVING, EACH JOINING IN AS YOU FEEL LED.

HEARING GOD

07

By this point, if you are like me, you are ready to start walking in the gifts of the Spirit! Before we get to this exciting and very natural part of life in the Kingdom, the Lord wants us to look at our very foundation.

READ 1 CORINTHIANS 13

If you've been to a wedding you've heard this passage, perhaps long before you gave your life to Christ. What you now realize (if you didn't before,) is this passage is sandwiched between Paul's two most significant teachings on the spiritual gifts! The Bible teaches us that God is love. Love is the reason for the gifts. The foundation of the Kingdom is love. It is summed up in the two greatest commands "Love the Lord your God with all your heart and with all your soul and with all your mind...and love your neighbor as yourself." The reason we didn't start with the gifts of the spirit in week one is because the gifts aren't the point. He is the point, and His people are the point. The gifts demonstrate that He is King and His Kingdom is at hand. God so loved the world that He gave...! He gave His all to us so we can give it away. In all of this He is honored if it is done in His love.

We love because He first loved us. The love comes from within and flows out like rivers of living water. Since we are temples of His Holy Spirit, we are governed by the Kingdom within. The river flows from the temple, from His Presence. When you encounter a river, it is very difficult to stop its path; so should it be with us. Whenever a circumstance, whether human or demonic, meets us, it should not be able to stop the flow of love. As Christ is formed in you, the river of God flowing from the inside creates this reality. Regardless of facts, we are governed by internal truth.

QUESTION:
WHAT IS LOVE IN GOD'S EYES? HOW ABOUT IN THE WORLD'S?

_____

_____

_____

_____

_____

_____

_____

So genuine love, flowing from within is a great measuring stick for the Spirit being formed in you. We need these gauges, to check ourselves as we step out. We also need accountability with the words we speak. If you are stepping out in prophecy, offer the Word in humility and take ownership if it does not come to pass. Although the Lord certainly speaks Words of admonishment, He is a grace machine. If the word does not build another person up, set it aside and pray extensively about it. There perhaps will be a perfect time to deliver the word in love, but often times it may not be the Lord and could cause real harm.

Then some elders of Israel came to me and sat down before me. And the word of the LORD came to me, saying, "Son of man, these men have set up their idols in their hearts and have put right before their faces the stumbling block of their iniquity. Should I be consulted by them at all? "Therefore speak to them and tell them, 'Thus says the Lord GOD, "Any man of the house of Israel who sets up his idols in his heart, puts right before his face the stumbling block of his iniquity, and then comes to the prophet, I the LORD will be brought to give him *an answer in the matter in view of the multitude of his idols, in order to lay hold of the hearts of the house of Israel who are estranged from Me through all their idols."'* **Ezekiel 14:1-5 NIV**

If we have an idol in our heart before the Lord He may answer us in keeping with our idolatry. For example, if your heart is turned towards money you may find yourself prophesying financial blessing over everyone you meet. David's prayer is a good one to help us remain circumspect so no evil root creeps up in us "Search me, God, and know my heart; test me and know my anxious thoughts. See if there is any offensive way in me..."

QUESTION:

• LORD, WHAT ARE THE IDOLS IN MY HEART THAT MAY AFFECT MY ABILITY TO HEAR YOU?

_____

_____

_____

_____

_____

_____

_____

_____

Journaling can be a very powerful tool (and daily discipline) to help commune with the Lord and capture His responses. Below is an abbreviated excerpt from Mark Viklers book on the 4 Keys to Hearing God's Voice that will help you with a practice of regularly hearing God.

4 Keys to Hearing God's Voice (by Mark Virkler)

I went to my office and reviewed what the Lord had been teaching me from **Habakkuk 2:1,2**: *"I will stand on my guard post and station myself on the rampart; And I will keep watch to see what He will speak to me...Then the Lord answered me and said, 'Record the vision....'"*
Habakkuk said, *"I will stand on my guard post..."* (**Hab. 2:1**).

The first key to hearing God's voice is to go to a quiet place and still our own thoughts and emotions.

Psalm 46:10 encourages us to be still, let go, cease striving, and know that He is God. In Psalm 37:7 we are called to "be still before the Lord and wait patiently for Him." There is a deep inner knowing in our spirits that each of us can experience when we quiet our flesh and our minds.

I have found that playing a worship song on my autoharp is the quickest way for me to come to stillness. I need to choose my song carefully; I choose gentle songs that express my love and worship. And it isn't enough just to sing the song into the cosmos – I come into the Lord's presence most quickly and easily when I use my godly imagination to see the truth that He is right here with me and I sing my songs to Him, personally.

If I fix my eyes upon Jesus (Heb. 12:2), the intuitive flow comes from Jesus. But if I fix my gaze upon some desire of my heart, the intuitive flow comes out of that desire. To have a pure flow I must become still and carefully fix my eyes upon Jesus. Quietly worshiping the King and receiving out of the stillness that follows quite easily accomplishes this.

So I used *the second key to hearing God's voice: As you pray, fix the eyes of your heart upon Jesus, seeing in the Spirit the dreams and visions of Almighty God*. Habakkuk was actually looking for vision as he prayed. He opened the eyes of his heart, and looked into the spirit world to see what God wanted to show him. You can see Christ present with you because Christ is present with you. In fact, the vision may come so easily that you will be tempted to reject it, thinking that it is just you. But if you persist in recording these visions, your doubt will soon be overcome by faith as you recognize that the content of them could only be birthed in Almighty God.

Like Habakkuk, I was coming to know the sound of God speaking to me (Hab. 2:2). Elijah described it as a still, small voice (I Kings 19:12). I had previously listened for an inner audible voice, and God does speak that way at times. However, I have found that usually, God's voice comes as spontaneous thoughts, visions, feelings, or impressions. For example, haven't you been driving down the road and had a thought come to you to pray for a certain person? Didn't you believe it was God telling you to pray? What did God's voice sound like? Was it an audible voice, or was it a spontaneous thought that lit upon your mind?

Experience indicates that we perceive spirit-level communication as spontaneous thoughts, impressions and visions, and Scripture confirms this in many ways. For example, one definition of *paga*, a Hebrew word for intercession, is "a chance encounter or an accidental intersecting." When God lays people on our hearts, He does it through *paga*, a chance-encounter thought "accidentally" intersecting our minds.

So *the third key to hearing God's voice is recognizing that God's voice in your heart often sounds like a flow of spontaneous thoughts*. Therefore, when I want to hear from God, I tune to chance-encounter or spontaneous thoughts. Finally, God told Habakkuk to record the vision (Hab. 2:2). This was not an isolated command. The Scriptures record many examples of individual's prayers and God's replies, such as the Psalms, many of the prophets, and Revelation. I have found that obeying this final principle amplified my confidence in my ability to hear God's voice so that I could finally make living out of His initiatives a way of life. The *fourth key, two-way journaling or the writing out of your prayers and God's answers, brings great freedom in hearing God's voice.*

I have found two-way journaling to be a fabulous catalyst for clearly discerning God's inner, spontaneous flow, because as I journal I am able to write in faith for long periods of time, simply believing it is God. I know that what I believe I have received from God must be tested. However, testing involves doubt and doubt blocks divine communication, so I do not want to test while I am trying to receive. (See James 1:5-8.) With journaling, I can receive in faith, knowing that when the flow has ended I can test and examine it carefully.

To learn to walk in the Spirit, which is the central them of the New Testament life in the Kingdom, we learn to allow God's love to flow in and through us. To help with this process we can develop new life-giving disciplines. These new disciplines bring supernatural revelation and will help us as we transition into learning about the gifts of the Spirit.

As you journal with God, He will constantly reaffirm your identity in Him. We must know who we are and from which place we pray. Jesus didn't pray weak, whiny prayers. He prayed from the place of identity. When He stood before the crowd outside of Lazarus' tomb, He prayed this, "Father I thank You that You hear Me. I knew that You always hear Me, but said this for a benefit of the people standing here, that they may believe You sent Me." (John 11:42) Jesus knew He was loved, and pleased the Lord. When we pray from that place of identity and authority, we see things shift. Jesus prayed the way He did so that those around Him would believe. He said at one point in His ministry, "Do not believe me unless I do the works of my Father." I believe the Father is looking for us to say the same thing and it starts with how we pray. We pray from the place of authority, knowing we are loved and bringing His will through us into the situations we will encounter as we step out in our spiritual gifts.

TO DO:

- PRACTICE TWO-WAY JOURNALING, ALLOWING GOD TO SPEAK TO YOUR IDENTITY USING THE 4 KEYS. HOLY SPIRIT, WHO DO YOU SAY I AM?

_____

_____

_____

_____

_____

_____

_____

_____

_____

_____

_____

_____

GROUP DISCUSSION:

- WHY IS IT IMPORTANT TO LEARN ABOUT LOVE BEFORE STEPPING OUT IN THE GIFTS OF THE SPIRIT?
- WHAT WERE YOUR MAJOR TAKEAWAYS WHEN LEARNING ABOUT THE 4 KEYS TO HEARING GOD'S VOICE?
- DID ANYONE HAVE A PARTICULARLY POWERFUL EXCHANGE WITH GOD IN YOUR JOURNALING?

_____

_____

_____

GROUP ACTIVITY:

- SEPARATE INTO GROUPS OF THREE AND SHARE YOUR TWO-WAY JOURNALING WITH EACH OTHER. SERVE AS THE "SECOND WITNESS" FOR ONE ANOTHER ON WHETHER THE JOURNALING SOUNDED LIKE THEY WERE INDEED HEARING GOD. IT'S OKAY TO MAKE MISTAKES HERE, WE ARE GROWING!

GIFTS OF THE SPIRIT

The Holy Spirit. It is the fire of God. Luke 3:16 John answered them all, *"I baptize you with water. But one who is more powerful than I will come... He will baptize you with the Holy Spirit and fire."* We do not have time to go into the full teaching, but the Scriptures lay out clearly that the baptism of the Spirit is separate and distinct from the baptism with water. The baptism of water cleanses and is symbolic of the dying of the old self and the rising of the new. The death and the resurrection.

Therefore we have been buried with Him through baptism into death, so that as Christ was raised from the dead through the glory of the Father, so we too might walk in newness of life. For if we have become united with Him in the likeness of His death, certainly we shall also be in the likeness of His resurrection, knowing this, that our old self was crucified with Him, in order that our body of sin might be done away with, so that we would no longer be slaves to sin; for he who has died is freed from sin. Now if we have died with Christ, we believe that we shall also live with Him. **Romans 6:4-8 NIV**

QUESTION:
- WHAT DOES PAUL MEAN BY THE 'LIKENESS OF HIS RESURRECTION' THAT I'M TO WALK IN?

_____

_____

_____

The symbolism of coming up from the water is rising to a new eternal life in Christ. This abundant life starts right away, but we have still dragged in our flesh. That flesh must be purified with fire. This is the baptism of fire John the Baptist referenced and the flames of fire we saw above each of their heads at Pentecost in Acts 2. They were being baptized by fire, and so must we. John 3:5 states "no one can enter the kingdom of God unless he is born of water and the Spirit." The fire is to burn us up, to eliminate our flesh that remains because we have already indeed died with Christ. The Spirit works on His behalf to sanctify our vessels so our temple can be Holy, Allowing Him to reside in us and move in power through us.

Revival history provides recent examples of what can happen when the Spirit comes with Power to sanctify vessels. Although the trembling, shaking and even falling has been controversial to the church at large, during every revival period it has happened. The "Quakers" didn't get their name for making oats. After Jesus was baptized even He was led by the Spirit into the wilderness for 40 days of prayer and fasting. Similar to the "quaking" some experience, if led by the Spirit, fasting does a similar work in dealing with the flesh. The fast and temptation ends in Luke 4:13, then verse 14 records Jesus returned to Galilee in the power of the Spirit. He came out with power! No words in scriptures are accidents, and this is the first time we see Him moving in what was noted as the power of the Spirit. So we learn the fast was essential. It was a work of the Spirit...and He came out with the Spirit's power. If we allow it, so shall we.

"Whoever believes in me will do the works I have been doing, and they will do even greater things than these, because I am going to the Father... And I will ask the Father, and he will give you another advocate to help you and be with you forever." **John 14:12, 16 NIV**

QUESTION:

- WHAT MAY BE HOLDING ME BACK FROM FULLY BELIEVING JESUS OWN WORDS ABOUT ME DOING GREATER WORKS THAN HE DID?

_____

_____

_____

The Spirit does His work inside of us and prepares us for the ministry of Jesus. Jesus came for a short while to show us how, made a way for all of us through His death and resurrection, then equipped us with His Spirit to do the same. This ministry will require us to develop our Spiritual senses. Often people will lump all of these senses into "hearing God," but hearing may not be the best word choice. God wants to use all of our senses to know Him and what He has for us at any given moment.

READ 1 CORINTHIANS 12:7-14

Notice how Paul expected this gathering of believers to walk in each of the gifts. It was an "all play" for their common good, to build each other up and to knit them together in unity. To increase their faith and to collectively experience transformational experiences. Here is a breakdown of the 9 gifts outlined:

Gifts to Say:
1. Prophecy
2. Tongues
3. Interpretation of Tongues

Gifts to Know:
1. Word of Wisdom
2. Word of Knowledge
3. Discerning of Spirits

Gifts to Do:
1. Gift of Faith
2. Gifts of Healing
3. Miraculous Powers

New body, new gifts! As new babes in the Kingdom how in the world can we expect to come out of the womb fully mature? The process to grow in our gifts will require patience and vulnerability, but our growth will forcefully advance the Kingdom! If we allow Him to work through our surrender we will ...*become mature, attaining to the whole measure of the fullness of Christ* **Eph 4:13 NIV**

It is the year 150 AD, your Legion of the Roman army has just received orders to conquer a new city, which is to become a stronghold for the region. You are brand new to the Legion, frankly everyone is. No one has trained. Not a single person in the unit has even used their weapons before. Although you have received orders from the Emperor of the greatest empire on earth, you are afraid. You wonder aloud why you are so afraid by asking a fellow Legionnaire. "Are you as nervous as I am?" "Yes" is his simple reply. "Do you know why? I mean, isn't victory assured for us?" "I don't want to die." The fellow legionnaire's answer resonates deep within. You realize you cannot enter this battle, even with victory assured, without preparation. You need to learn how to use your weapons. You don't want fear to stand in the way between you and your destiny. Especially when that fear can be mitigated with some training. After all, you have more manpower, superior equipment and far more resources than the city you are entering. You further realize you have intelligence and will know just when to attack. Your confidence grows. You decide to approach the centurion. "Would it be okay if we did a bit of training out here before we attack? I will help!" Your reasonable request is granted. You now begin to train with the unfamiliar weapons. You quickly learn anyone can learn how to use them, because your weapons are superior. Let's start training together on the weapons that will help us usher in the victory that has already been assured by the One who is faithful.

QUESTION:

WHAT IS SOMETHING I'VE TRAINED A LOT FOR? WHAT WAS MY COMFORT LEVEL WHEN THE ACTUAL EVENT ARRIVED? CONTRAST THAT WITH SOMETHING YOU WERE ASKED TO DO BUT NEVER TRAINED FOR.

_____

_____

_____

Prophecy

"The Gift of Prophecy is the special ability that God gives to members of the Body of Christ to receive and communicate an immediate message of God to His gathered people, a group among them, or any one of His people individually, through a divinely anointed utterance" **David Pytches**.

The Greek word for prophecy, "propheteia," implies that one is speaking for another; speaking on behalf of God. Paul encourages us to specifically desire to prophesy in 1 Corinthians 14.

Tongues

"The Gift of Tongues is the supernatural ability to speak to others and/or to God in a language or utterance never learned by the speaker" **Dr. Bill Bright, Campus Crusade for Christ**

There can be three types:
1. When coupled with The Gift of Interpretation, Tongues can operate similarly to Prophecy, building up the body.
2. Tongues can also be expressing praise to God, and therefore any interpretation is also in terms of prayer, praise or thanksgiving to God Himself.
3. The Gift of Tongues can also be another earthly language. In Acts 2 we see how uneducated men were speaking languages and "all heard in their native language."

Interpretation of Tongues

The word "interpretation" here is from the Greek "harmeneia" meaning "explanation" or "full interpretation." It is the ability through the inspiration of the Holy Spirit to bring understandable meaning to an inspired public message in tongues. It is often a Spirit-inspired declaration of praise, exaltation and honoring of God Himself. If the language spoken is an earthly one, however, there is often someone present who speaks the language and can interpret.

Word of Wisdom

Wisdom is the right application of knowledge. The Word of Wisdom gives us the skill in knowing how and when to minister accurately by the Holy Spirit into peoples' lives. It makes the timing right and enables the other Gifts to make a significant impact.

Word of Knowledge

The revelation of facts past, present or future which were not learned through the efforts of the natural mind. To bring supernatural encouragement, to give confirmation to what God has already been saying or doing, to give insight and understanding of what is ahead in the purposes of God, to help in counselling/evangelistic situations, to unlock hindrances to healing/unanswered prayers, to give strategies in spiritual warfare, to reveal where sin is being covered up, to open up a meeting or situation for God to move.

Discerning of Spirits

The Gift of Discerning of Spirits allows the believer to know what is in operation in a person, church or even geographical area. *"The Gift that gives the Christian insight into the supernatural world. The Gift is to enable the person to know the motivation behind a situation or person"* **Rev. Alistair Taylor**.

Gift of Faith

The Gift of Faith is supernatural, and Spirit led because it defies all earthly logic and reason. A sudden feeling of knowing that God is able to do abundantly more than we ask or think is a signal of the Gift of Faith. The late John Wimber describes it as "The mysterious surge of confidence which sometimes arises within a person faced with a specific situation or need."

Gifts of Healing

The Gifts of Healing can range from the Spirit bringing healing to one ailment in a person to supernaturally to healing physical, spiritual and emotional and making a person whole in the fullest sense of the word. Jesus works of healing through the Holy Spirit were complete in nature, making the person whole in every way. Healing was a vital part of Jesus' ministry. He taught His disciples to follow His example. It should be an ordinary part of our lives and ministries.

Miraculous Powers

"A remarkable or surprising event that happens by the direct intervention of God, not following the general known laws of nature" **Dr. David Yonggi Cho, South Korea**. This Gift is desperately needed to impact an unbelieving church and world!

That is a brief summary of each of the 9 gifts of the Spirit. Next week we will take a deeper look into how each of these gifts tend to operate. Before we complete this section, it is important to clear up one common misconception. That is the misunderstanding that people only get one gift! We did not get a partial Holy Spirit. The same Spirit that raised Christ from the dead lives in us. It takes time to develop into the fullness of Christ as Paul describes, but all the gifts are available and as you grow you can operate in different gifts at different times as the Spirit sees fit. This is particularly important to remember as you operate in the gifts in your small group. There are 9 gifts of the Spirit, how cool would it be if all 9 were on display in your group through different participants! This functioning is designed to be an ALL PLAY, and non-participation by someone in the group could cause the group to miss something additional and awesome the Lord would like to do among you. All of that stated, 1 Corinthians 12 makes it clear that all do not operate in all the spiritual gifts in a single meeting – so never expect a single person to operate in all the gifts in a gathering.

QUESTION:

- HOLY SPIRIT, WHEN WERE THE TIMES I OPERATED IN THE GIFTS WITHOUT EVEN REALIZING IT?

GROUP DISCUSSION:

- WHEN WERE SOME MOMENTS YOU FEEL LIKE YOU OPERATED IN A GIFT OF THE SPIRIT? HAS ANYONE EVER USED A GIFT OF THE SPIRIT WITH YOU? WHAT HAVE BEEN YOUR THOUGHTS OR PRECONCEPTIONS ABOUT THE GIFTS OF THE SPIRIT?

GROUP ACTIVITY:

- SEPARATE INTO GROUPS OF FOUR AND DESIGNATE ONE PERSON AT A TIME TO PRAY FOR. GET QUIET AND PRACTICE THE 4 KEYS TO HEARING GOD AND WRITE THE WORDS/IMAGES/IMPRESSIONS GOD GIVES YOU FOR THE PERSON. TAKE TURNS SHARING THOSE WORDS, ASKING FOR FURTHER WISDOM/INTERPRETATION AS YOU DO.

The basis for the overview of the gifts has been taken from "Spiritual Gifts" (by Alistair Taylor), International Bible Institute of London, U.K. and developed by Pastor Rodney W. Francis (New Zealand)

GIFTS OF THE SPIRIT

09

Last week we reviewed each of the gifts of the Spirit. This week we will look at some Biblical examples of how they can be used. Before we dive in, let's acknowledge that a childlike faith and willingness to fail and even look foolish is a part of the learning process (which will last the rest of our lives.) Death to self is truly needed to step into this realm and remain. Jesus Himself gave a cry of His heart in Luke 18:8 saying "...when the Son of Man comes, will He find faith on the earth?" We find Jesus constantly rebuking His disciples for not having faith, and then He expresses this concern for all of us to see. We know from Hebrews 12 that a good Father disciplines those He loves, but what is the reason for the rebuke or discipline? It is to spurn us on to more growth. Like a coach throwing down a challenge to a player, I sense the Lord saying "go for it! If you're not failing you're not stretching yourself enough! Trust Me, have faith, take risk and do the things I did!" With that, let's explore the gifts of the Spirit applied in scripture.

Prophecy, Tongues & Interpretation of Tongues – The "Saying" Gifts

READ 1 COR 14:2-28

This is a great passage on how the gifts work in a gathering to build up the body. How encouraging! This sounds like a very exciting and uplifting gathering. He certainly encourages the use of both tongues and prophecy and notes how tongues communicate with God and are great for building up your Spirit, but since prophecy builds up the body in gatherings it is preferred. He says do both, but have an interpreter for the tongues...and prophecy as much as you can! Throughout the gospels, we see Jesus not only fulfilling prophecy, but prophesying about His death, His resurrection, the future destruction of the temple and much more. In Acts 1 we see the apostles casting lots (kind of like rolling Holy dice!) to see who would replace Judas, but after receiving the Holy Spirit they look to Him for prophetic insights for the important decisions.

One of them named Agabus stood up and began to indicate by the Spirit that there would certainly be a great famine all over the world. And this took place in the reign of Claudius. And in the proportion that any of the disciples had means, each of them determined to send a contribution for the relief of the brethren living in Judea. And this they did, sending it in charge of Barnabas and Saul to the elders. **Acts 11:28-30 NIV**

Notice in the passage how they acted in faith upon the prophecy of Agabus. They took up a collection right there on the spot for something that hadn't even happened yet! We later see Agabus prophesying Paul's future trouble in Jerusalem in Acts 21 by tying himself up with Paul's belt. The Holy Spirit spoke a Word of prophecy about sending Paul and Barnabas after a time of fasting and worship. In Acts 27 Paul accurately prophecies the voyage would be of great loss to ship and cargo. There are many other occasions in the Old and New Testaments of the Holy Spirit speaking prophetic Words through regular people filled with the Spirit.

Back in the 1 Corinthians 14 passage, Paul says *I speak in tongues more than you all.* He notes tongues are great for "personal edification," so it sounds like Paul builds up his Spiritual man through both singing and speaking in tongues (which he also calls tongues of angels in 1 Cor 13.) At Pentecost we see a different type of tongue, however.

READ ACTS 2:4-11

Here at the initial outpouring of the Holy Spirit we see uneducated men speaking in foreign languages "so all could understand in his own language." The form of tongues at this initial outpouring was clearly a productive sign and wonder as the tongues announced the glory and power of God to all in attendance.

READ ACTS 19:1-7

This group was actually noted as being disciples, but had not received the Holy Spirit. So Paul laid hands on them and they immediately began speaking in tongues and prophesying.

Ultimately Paul ends his very helpful dialogue on the edifying interplay between prophecy, tongues and interpretation in 1 Cor 14:39-40 *with Therefore, my brethren, desire earnestly to prophesy, and do not forbid to speak in tongues. But all things must be done properly and in an orderly manner.*

QUESTION:
- HOLY SPIRIT, WHAT DO YOU WANT TO TEACH ME ABOUT TONGUES (PRAYING IN THE SPIRIT?)

_____

_____

_____

_____

There are numerous wonderful stories about the saying gifts in operation now. One of my favorites comes from Gateway Church pastor Robert Morris in his book about the Holy Spirit titled "The God I Never Knew." In this book Robert details his personal long standing struggle with watching things he wasn't supposed to be watching. In the story, his most recent bout with the problem arose in his hotel room one night the weekend he was leading a prophetic conference! The next day he woke up and felt an awful remorse, but also noticed he was struggling to hear from the Lord. Not a good combo when you're leading a prophetic conference! That very morning a young man on his team who had never spoken announced he had a Word from the Lord to share with everyone. Since Robert wasn't hearing so well and was feeling so bad he happily agreed to let the young man take the lead. His word...was on someone struggling with watching impure things that was ready to change. He said "if you humble yourself and come to the altar the Lord will deliver you." You got it! Pastor Morris did something 99.9% of people in his position probably would NOT do. He knew it was the Lord so he humbled himself and came to the altar. After that, he said he was set free and never struggled in that area again.

Word of Wisdom, Word of Knowledge, Discerning of Spirits – The "Knowing" Gifts

Jesus said He only did what He saw the Father doing, so He only spoke what He heard the Father speaking. This allowed Him to utter profound Words of both knowledge and wisdom throughout His ministry. In doing so, He demonstrated for us what it looks like to speak when led by the Spirit. There are so many stories to pick from you can read any gospel and see a Word of Wisdom from Jesus. Here is an example.

They answered Him, "We are Abraham's descendants and have never yet been enslaved to anyone; how is it that You say, 'You will become free'?" Jesus answered them, "Truly, truly, I say to you, everyone who commits sin is the slave of sin. "The slave does not remain in the house forever; the son does remain forever. "So if the Son makes you free, you will be free indeed. **John 8:33-36 NIV**

This group of Pharisees confess they are sons of Abraham and have never been slaves (as an aside, it appears this group of Pharisees did not even descend from Jacob and the 12 tribes, since they confess their people were never slaves in Egypt!) Using a Word of wisdom Jesus hits right at the heart of the matter. These men were indeed slaves...to sin. A Word of wisdom from God often looks beyond the surface discussion and goes for the heart. Let's look at Jesus using a Word of Knowledge.

When they came to Capernaum, those who collected the two-drachma tax came to Peter and said, "Does your teacher not pay the two-drachma tax?" He said, "Yes." And when he came into the house, Jesus spoke to him first, saying, "What do you think, Simon? From whom do the kings of the earth collect customs or poll-tax, from their sons or from strangers?" When Peter said, "From strangers," Jesus said to him, "Then the sons are exempt. "However, so that we do not offend them, go to the sea and throw in a hook, and take the first fish that comes up; and when you open its mouth, you will find a shekel.

Take that and give it to them for you and Me." **Matthew 17:24-27 NIV**

In this story Peter is asked if they were going to pay the temple tax. Although they didn't have to, they complied. Using a profound Word of Knowledge (and working of a miracle,) Jesus tells the fisherman to do what he does best to find the money. There is perhaps a deeper lesson in this one for all of us, which we will leave for another day.

As for the discerning of Spirits, In Matt 16:21 Jesus rebuked Peter by saying "get behind me satan" when Peter insisted Jesus would never suffer and die. Jesus rebuked his disciples for not being able to discern that prayer and fasting was required for the type of spirit that was seizing the boy in Mark 9. The knowing gifts weren't just limited to Jesus. Remember the story about Ananias and Saphira from Acts 5? Peter "knew" Saphira was going to be struck dead as well.

QUESTION:

- HOW DO YOU EXPECT IT WOULD CHANGE YOU TO BE USED BY GOD IN SUCH A WAY?

_____

_____

_____

These gifts can have a dramatic impact on people's lives as you use them to minister. Recently I was having breakfast with a friend from church and we decided to pray and ask God for a Word for our waitress. As we did my friend immediately got a name. When the waitress returned, we asked if the name meant anything to her. As her entire countenance changed to a look of shock upon hearing, the Lord gave me additional revelation about her situation. She had been battling with an ex-husband and it was taking a toll on her both physically and emotionally. As we assured her that the Lord knew her pain and wanted to hold her hand through the process, she wept. We walked away knowing the Lord used us. He profoundly shifted the course of someone's life simply because we asked and my friend heard. She now knew He was both real and that He loved and cared for her.

These "knowing" gifts can even be used for personal edification. For example, yesterday the Lord showed me a locomotive with a cloud of smoke coming out of the engine. As I inquired I received an instruction to look up the word and I came to its Latin root, which meant "pertaining to movement from a place." I then received a Word of wisdom (often called an interpretation) that God is moving me forward in the cloud of His Presence. This was a very reassuring Word that was confirmed in my Spirit and built me up.

"Activation" of the gifts of the Spirit require not only hearing, but awareness and sensitivity. It is very difficult to sense what God is doing when you're busy or if there is pressure. As we move forward to group exercises in practicing the gifts, shift to a posture of rest (since it's all up to Him anyway) and pay attention to everything going on in your body. The Holy Spirit will often use very subtle and acute sensations to cue you in on an opportunity. It's truly a "Spiritual sense." Why? Well, for one He has all of our physical senses to work with (sight, hearing, touch, smell and taste) and many believe our Spirits have all of these senses as well.

If we are being led by our physical senses all the time we are called "sensual." So we must learn to use our Spiritual senses as we mature in Christ, and this is a process. Why does God prefer to use something so subtle? Possibly to draw us closer to Him and His mystery, but remember He used massive miracles with Israel as they left the promise land, yet they all perished in their unbelief! So if you are ministering and suddenly get a scent, inquire of the Lord! If you see a written word, inquire of the Lord for an interpretation. Same with even tasting something unique. You will often find as you share what you are experiencing from the Lord with the person you are ministering to the Lord will fill your mouth with the Word of wisdom to connect the dots. It's beautiful and builds both of you up!

Gift of Faith, Gifts of Healing, Miraculous Powers – The "Doing" Gifts

I love Jesus' message when sending out the 12 for the first time in Matthew 10. It's a message for all of us. "*As you go, proclaim this message: 'The kingdom of heaven has come near.' Heal the sick, raise the dead, cleanse those who have leprosy, drive out demons. Freely you have received; freely give.*" If you are wondering what the Lord's will is for your life, well there you have it. This instruction covers all of the doing gifts. We saw Jesus do it all of this and more in His ministry, then we see the apostles doing the same. Luke 9 adds a little detail to what happened on this first mission trip: *So they set out and went from village to village, proclaiming the good news and healing people everywhere.* They did it! And so can you.

READ ACTS 3:1-10

This story is one of many examples of the apostles operating in the "doing" gifts. They had the gift of faith it would happen and the miraculous healing happened. We see the gift of faith on display throughout the Bible with David running toward Goliath, Joshua commanding the sun to stand still and Daniel in the Lion's Den to name a few. Peter walking on water is a great example of the gift of faith combining with a miracle. These gifts are often packaged together as it takes the faith to declare something that you don't have much natural confidence will happen!

In order to step into the supernatural you truly have to be childlike in your trust and foolish to the world around you. One modern example of the gift of faith we've always loved in our family was of my great grandfather Dr. Max Wertheimer. Grandpa Max was a rabbi that gave his life to Christ and became a minister. Although he was busy with speaking engagements, they had long stretches of time with little money. One morning they found themselves flat broke and without breakfast, so they decided to pray. While praying for a breakfast that wasn't even in front of them, a farmer down the road knocked on the door asking if they would like some fresh eggs and bread.
John 6:63 effectively sums up what we are walking into. The Spirit alone gives life. Human effort accomplishes nothing. And the very words I have spoken to you are spirit and life. We conquer with the Words and information the Spirit is giving us, not with our own "willing it to happen." Human effort accomplishes nothing. We find these signs and wonders followed the apostles everywhere they brought the message of the Kingdom, and Jesus wants us to walk in the same level of fullness. Let's walk with Him as He grows us up in these gifts.

QUESTION:
- HOLY SPIRIT, WHAT ELSE DO YOU WANT TO SAY TO ME ABOUT YOUR GIFTS?

_____

_____

_____

_____

_____

_____

_____

_____

_____

_____

_____

_____

_____

_____

GROUP DISCUSSION:
- WHAT DO YOU FEEL HOLDS YOU BACK FROM EMBRACING THE GIFTS?

GROUP DISCUSSION:
- PRAY OVER EACH OTHER TO BREAK ANY "FEAR OF MAN" IN OPERATION BEFORE GETTING STARTED WITH MINISTRY TIME. SITTING IN A CIRCLE (OR MANNER IN WHICH EVERYONE CAN PARTICIPATE) AND OPERATING FROM A TOTAL PLACE OF REST (NO PRESSURE TO PERFORM,) INVITE THE PRESENCE OF THE HOLY SPIRIT TO MINISTER AMONG YOU AND SHARPEN YOUR SENSES TO HIS ACTIVITY. AS SOMEONE GETS A WORD OR SENSITIVITY IN THEIR BODY OR SPIRITUAL MIND, ANNOUNCE IT. MINISTER TO THE PERSON THE WORD OR SENSING WAS FOR, THEN REPEAT AND ALLOW THE SPIRIT TO LEAD.

FUNCTIONING AS A BODY USING THE GIFTS

10

The gifts are amazing, but they are only part of being in the Kingdom. We must not elevate them above having a relationship with Jesus, but recognize they are a benefit of our relationship. As we operate in the gifts to minister to others, we see His amazing love for people and we are personally built up with confidence in what Jesus is doing in the world. With that stated, let's be very practical as we proceed. We see these gifts, collectively referred to as "signs and wonders," on display everywhere the Kingdom was preached as the early church advanced. The skepticism and bondage in people's lives is no less today, and perhaps much greater, so how much more the need for these to accompany our efforts today? But will we run a play in a game if we haven't drilled it in practice? Rather once we have mastered the play in practice, then we will run it in the game with confidence. Such is the case with the gifts. We must first learn together, functioning as a body ministering to one another and allowing the Spirit to build our confidence with every step.

John Wimber, founder of the Vineyard movement used to say "everybody gets to play." If we are His, we get to advance His Kingdom using the gifts. This is in contrast to a mindset that has hindered our progress. That mindset is to "leave it to the pros" and refer anyone with a need to the pastoral staff, causing everyone else to have an almost inactive role in ministry. This approach has hindered much of the work of the Kingdom and runs directly contrary to Jesus' own teachings. Jesus summed up His stance on elevating men by instructing.

"But do not be called Rabbi; for One is your Teacher, and you are all brothers. Do not call anyone on earth your father; for One is your Father, He who is in heaven. Do not be called leaders; for One is your Leader, that is, Christ. "But the greatest among you shall be your servant. Whoever exalts himself shall be humbled; and whoever humbles himself shall be exalted." **Matthew 23:8-12 NIV**

QUESTION:

• HOW DO OUR CURRENT STRUCTURES FIT WITH THESE WORDS FROM JESUS?

_____

_____

_____

_____

_____

_____

_____

_____

_____

People need to see "regular folks" walking in the power of the Spirit, being salt and light. As His co-heirs, we are ALL called off the bench and into "full time ministry." As we take our steps in this transition we must learn to function as a body, serving and lifting one another up. We will be practicing the gifts in a safe environment so we know we have them. We will step out in risk.
Let's look at Paul's description of the gifts working in a body.

READ 1 COR INTHIANS 12:12-31

We are one body. Could you imagine waking up to find that one of your body parts decided not to participate for the day? Or how about if one decided to run the entire show? Either would lead to a very bad day. Now put this in context when we gather. Paul is painting a picture that will allow us to see a fuller picture of Christ. Mutual participation using the gifts of the Spirit.

His intent was that now, through the church, the manifold wisdom of God should be made known to the rulers and authorities in the heavenly realms.
Ephesians 3:10 NIV

The Greek word for manifold used here is Polypoikilos (much varied, marked with a great variety of colors, of a painting.) Our mutual participation is a brilliant display of many facets of God's wisdom. A painting with one color can be beautiful, but how much more so with a great variety of colors!? Remember, this display is both for us and for the rulers in the heavenly realms! When only one person speaks, we only see one reflection of God's wisdom. How then do we all participate to see His manifold wisdom on display? We honor each other, allowing each to share what God is showing them as we pray in the Spirit together. This can and should be orderly. We test the Words to confirm they do not run contrary to anything in His written Word and we ask the Spirit in each of us for confirmation as a second witness. There is clearly much discovery as a part of this process, but one of our primary joys in this life (and the life to come) should be discovery.

"It is the glory of God to conceal a matter; to search out a matter is the glory of kings." **Proverbs 25:2 NIV**

Did you enjoy 'hide and seek' as a child? How about following the clues on a scavenger hunt? We have learned the Lord sees us as His Kings and Priests unto Him, so this verse is personal. This verse is our destiny. It holds the key to unlock what it means to function in the gifts together. It is about discovery! The world has long celebrated the "self-made man" and independence, but the Lord is teaching us the beauty and art of interdependence. As we depend on the Holy Spirit operating through one another, we learn to celebrate Him and each other. It literally helps us fulfill His summary of all the laws and commands (Love God, Love each other.) Praise God He has indeed given us a helper to guide us in this discovery process together!

QUESTION:
     • WHAT IS THE HOLY SPIRIT SAYING TO ME?

_____

_____

_____

_____

_____

_____

_____

_____

_____

_____

_____

_____

_____

_____

_____

_____

GROUP DISCUSSION:

- WHAT IS INTERDEPENDENCE?
- WHAT WERE SOME MOMENTS IN YOUR LIFE WHEN YOU FELT GENUINE INTERDEPENDENCE WITH A TEAM OR ANOTHER PERSON? WHAT WOULD IT BE LIKE TO FEEL THAT WITH EACH OTHER?

_____

_____

_____

_____

GROUP ACTIVITY:

- PRAYER TO BREAK THE FEAR OFF ONE ANOTHER AS WE STEP OUT IN PRACTICE. SITTING IN A CIRCLE (OR MANNER IN WHICH EVERYONE CAN PARTICIPATE) AND OPERATING FROM A TOTAL PLACE OF REST (NO PRESSURE TO PERFORM,) INVITE THE PRESENCE OF THE HOLY SPIRIT TO MINISTER AMONG YOU AND SHARPEN YOUR SENSES TO HIS ACTIVITY. AS SOMEONE GETS A WORD OR SENSITIVITY IN THEIR BODY OR SPIRITUAL MIND, ANNOUNCE IT. MINISTER TO THE PERSON THE WORD OR SENSING WAS FOR, THEN REPEAT AND ALLOW THE SPIRIT TO LEAD. I ENCOURAGE YOU TO USE MORE BOLDNESS AS YOU MINISTER THIS TIME, REMEMBERING JESUS ASKING "WILL I FIND ANY FAITH WHEN I COME BACK?" AS A CHALLENGE.

_____

_____

_____

_____

DISCIPLESHIP

Christian author Mike Arnold retells a story about an encounter with a donor in his book titled Uprising. Mike's ministry has a preference of going deep into long periods of discipleship with a smaller number of people, but the donor was used to seeing large numbers of conversions from the ministries he supports. Struggling to make headway with the donor, Mike asked the Holy Spirit for help. At that moment, he felt the Spirit say "run the numbers."

After the meeting Mike did exactly that. He used generous estimates suggesting if he started a new ministry to fulfill PART of the great commission and it grew by 1,000 new "decisions for Christ" each year (20 new people every Sunday) with a 25% retention rate. Now say he could do this for just $100,000 a year AND he could set up 100,000 identical ministries around the globe that could reproduce the same numbers. This would be amazing, right? These are numbers many ministries would dream about! Now let's say it were truly doable and reproducible. How long would it take to reach every man, woman and child on the earth? Even if the earth's population were to stop growing, it would take 280 years and $2,800,000,000,000.00. Add in population growth and there would be nearly 3x as many people born each year than we could ever reach. Ouch!

"All authority in heaven and on earth has been given to me. Therefore go and make disciples of all nations, baptizing them in the name of the Father and of the Son and of the Holy Spirit, and teaching them to obey everything I have commanded you. And surely I am with you always, to the very end of the age." **Matthew 28:18-20 NIV**

Now Mike contrasts that, a strategy being implemented almost across the board in the body of Christ currently, with one more similar to what Jesus demonstrated for us. The primary goal of this new ministry would be to live a life that reflects Christ. Over time five people are drawn to the fruit of the Spirit in your life and ask how you have so much joy. Now let's say you spend the next three years pouring into these five until Christ is really formed in their lives. After these three years, the six of you go out and do the same, rolling this forward every three years with each person added. How long would it take in this scenario for the full great commission (making disciples) to be fulfilled? Less than 39 years! That is with population growth and puts you 2 billion beyond your goal of every man, woman and child on earth. The cost: zero dollars!

QUESTON:
- WHAT IS THE HOLY SPIRIT SAYING TO ME?
- ARE THERE FIVE PEOPLE I SENSE THE LORD ENCOURAGING ME TO SPEND MORE TIME WITH AS I GROW?

_____

_____

_____

_____

_____

_____

_____

_____

_____

Does the enemy want the body of Christ to recognize this opportunity? Certainly not! Instead, he wants us to live in a very small story, kind of like our dog Megan. Megan spends her days in a small space in our home with the occasional walk down our street. She doesn't know much different, so she is happy as long as she gets her little treats each day. She loves to spend time with us, her breakfast and dinner, the walks and getting her little doggie bites. In fact, her instincts for the doggie bites are so strong she forsakes the greatest desire of her heart (spending time with us.) So when it's time for her to go to bed at night, we have to coax her into her room so we can close the door. Without calling out "treat" this would be impossible. Megan would fight, fuss or run rather than go in that room! But when she gets close enough and we put out that treat, she willingly walks right in, following her nose and stomach every single time! I always wonder what her feeling is when that door closes behind us. "Rats! Fell for it again." The other day I got a picture of this being the Christian life many of us live. Really small lives that lack vision because we're simply living for our little treats. The enemy is all too happy to play into our small stories, offering us treats and closing the door behind us, with a plan to use the same tricks to do it all over again day after day. Unlike dogs, we have the ability to open the door. If we lack vision of how the Lord is calling us into our role in His great Story, as co-heirs in His Kingdom, I'm afraid the enemy's tricks will continue to work on us.

...in order that Satan might not outwit us. For we are not unaware of his schemes. **2 Cor 2:11 NIV**

If we are in genuine, vulnerable discipleship relationships, surrendering our lives so that Christ can be formed in us, we will be aware of the devil's schemes. Why? Because we will be airing the lies in our heads to one another, gaining intel on the accuser and enemy of our souls. In his famous 1942 work 'The Screwtape Letters,' Christian author C.S. Lewis wrote a book from the enemy perspective. In the book Screwtape, an experienced tempter in Hell guides a less experienced tempter (Wormwood) in his effort to draw his assigned patient away from the Enemy (God) and into the Underworld (Hell). Here are three quotes from the book that are profound and helpful as we plan to step out.

Indeed the safest road to Hell is the gradual one—the gentle slope, soft underfoot, without sudden turnings, without milestones, without signposts...

It is funny how mortals always picture us as putting things into their minds: in reality our best work is done by keeping things out.

These quotes are shared as a warning. The enemy has studied mankind for almost 6,000 years and developed strategies to thwart Christian initiative for the past 2,000 years. We need to be circumspect, aware, and sharing the dialogue in our heads with other "ALL IN" disciples so the lies can be dismantled. The enemy strategy to distort Truth has always been the same.

"...for there is no truth in him. When he lies, he speaks his native language, for he is a liar and the father of lies." **John 8:44 NIV**

If we are in these relationships and we do fall, we will not fall victim to the lies again. Where the Spirit of the Lord is there is freedom. We did not receive a Spirit that deserts us when we fall short. The definition of sin is "missing the mark." Christ's sacrifice was sufficient to cover us for good. Sometimes we need that reminder, who better from than the ones we are called to transparent and vulnerable relationships with.

Two are better than one, because they have a good return for their labor: If either of them falls down, one can help the other up. But pity anyone who falls and has no one to help them up. **Ecclesiastes 4:9-10 NIV**

For though the righteous fall seven times, they rise again... **Proverbs 24:16 NIV**

This is a call to discipleship as our reasonable next step. To form groups, operate in the gifts and to meet with one another until Christ is formed in us and the Kingdom is advanced all around us. There are some brilliant strategies in the body right now on this very topic. In their book "Contagious Discipleship," father and son disciple makers David and Paul Watson provide one of the best examples I've seen through forming what they call "Disciple Making Movements." I highly recommend this book. If you don't have time to read, simply google "discovery Bible study." Your search results will provide you with many resources on how to host a Bible study for any small size group that allows the Holy Spirit to lead. With the Spirit as the leader, these groups can multiply quickly and enable discipleship relationships to flourish!

QUESTION:

- IS THERE ANYTHING HOLDING ME BACK FROM ENTERING INTO DISCIPLESHIP RELATIONSHIPS? HOW CAN THESE OBSTACLES BE ELIMINATED?

_____

_____

_____

_____

_____

_____

GROUP DISCUSSION:

- WHAT WERE YOUR THOUGHTS ABOUT THE TWO CONTRASTING MINISTRY MODELS? WHAT MINISTRY MODEL DO YOU FEEL THE LORD MODELED? HOW REALISTIC IS IT FOR YOU TO BE IN MULTIPLE DISCIPLESHIP RELATIONSHIPS? WHAT ARE THE REWARDS OF BEING IN THESE RELATIONSHIPS? ARE THERE ANY REASONS WE SHOULD NOT BE IN ONGOING, INTENTIONAL DISCIPLESHIP RELATIONSHIPS? IT WOULD BE GREAT IF SOMEONE BROUGHT IN AN EXAMPLE DISCOVERY BIBLE STUDY TO BRIEFLY GO THROUGH TOGETHER.

GROUP ACTIVITY:

- BREAK INTO GROUPS OF TWO. DISCUSS WITH YOUR PARTNER WHAT PEOPLE YOU FEEL THE LORD IS CALLING YOU TO ENTER INTO DISCIPLESHIP RELATIONSHIPS WITH. WHAT ARE SOME OBSTACLES YOU NEED TO GET BEYOND TO DO SO? HOW ARE YOU GOING TO GET STARTED? HOW WILL YOU CHECK IN ON ONE ANOTHER TO PROVIDE UPDATES AND ENCOURAGE EACH OTHER?

WHAT'S AHEAD

12

Earlier we discussed how the primary work of the Holy Spirit is to "burn us up," with the end goal of making our whole temple Holy as He is Holy. No flesh enters in, so the flesh blindfolds we are wearing on this earth have to be dealt with. When you think about it, every spiritual practice is illogical from a human perspective. Tithing, serving, prayer, fasting and worship all require faith, because they demonstrate a dependence on God to meet our needs rather than securing them ourselves. Is our goal to get great at these spiritual practices, or is there even a higher calling as we live out the days of our pilgrimage on earth?

READ JOHN 17:20-26

QUESTION:
• WHAT IS JESUS SAYING IN THIS PASSAGE?

_____

_____

_____

_____

_____

John 17:20-26 is the very end of Jesus' longest unbroken message in the gospels. It is literally the crescendo of a message and prayer that goes back almost five chapters. Upon finishing this last prayer, Jesus will be taken captive. So let's just say this is THE major thing on His heart. What is His heart's cry? That we would be ONE! That we would be truly connected. It's the oneness the first church enjoyed where they ate together and prayed together in unity and the Lord added to their number every day. Healthy things grow. Being so deeply connected to Him and each other is His heart's greatest desire, and the world's greatest need. It's literally what we were made for. His original intent expresses it (let's make man in our image,) His design of family displays it (they will leave their father and mother and become one flesh,) the greatest commandment (Love Him, Love each other) demonstrates it and our hearts cry out for it (to know and be fully known.) Of course, the adversary of all things God wants opposes it, perverting everything that brings unity into our lives (the holiness of His temple with sin, the sanctity of marriage with adultery and divorce, our love for Him and others with selfishness.) But His Spirit in us is greater. It cries out Abba Father, and He is faithful to lead us in the connection and vulnerability with Him and others we were made for.

Let's enjoy this journey as the Lord gives us vision and pours out His love on us. Let's treat every day as a blank canvas for Him to paint a masterpiece on. His Kingdom is the kingdom of this world but "upside down." If you want to be great, be a servant. If you want joy, give it away first. If you need to be lifted up, lift Him up. Literally, whatever you want or need in this life first must be given away. It's His principle. Living this way allows us to live lighter, live free and enjoy the adventure with others.

Keep on taking risk! Be like a child as you step out in the supernatural Kingdom life and be willing to do the unusual. The most important thing in this life isn't what others think of you or what you do, but who He is in you. Stepping out where only He can come through will allow you to see into this beautiful mystery. Dream with God and embrace the pictures He gives you. These dreams and visions will keep you from living a small, insignificant life and literally pull you right into your destiny. The dreams should always involve people, because His people are His purpose for us. Be patient and forgiving of yourself during this process though! Building genuine character takes time. How much time did it take for you to be conformed to the pattern of this world? Years of TV, internet, being with people who love the things of this world, etc. So much more having your mind renewed. Transformation is a process, be patient with it. It requires surrender, so give each day to Him and invest your time rather than spending it.

READ REV 22:1-5

Eden is restored my friends. Even now, in Christ we are as if we never ate the fruit. The tree of life was guarded in the garden after the fall, but in John 15 Jesus said I am the true vine. Jesus has undone the curse. Intimacy and relationship with the Lord releases authority to bring His healing to the nations. I pray that you will be awakened to the authority you possess as you abide in Him. That you will move past all barriers and obstacles in your own life and begin to shift cities, regions, and nations with your God-given authority one disciple at a time. His living water is meant to not just flow into you, but through you.

The enemy has too long lulled the world of Christianity into inactivity and slumber through religious doctrines that promote fear and a "bunker" mentality. Too many sermons and too much of our "end times" theology is based on a fictitious storyline that hinges on a few verses that have a different meaning when you go deeper into the text and context. What has been the resulting fruit? Hunker down, stock up, get ready for the enemy to reign until the Lord returns! Did Christ demonstrate what it looks like to conquer and charge us to do the same to the ends of the earth for us to hide and play it safe?

QUESTION:
- WHAT ENDTIME CHRISTIAN WORLDVIEW HAVE I BELIEVED?
- WHAT HAS BEEN THE FRUIT OF THIS IN MY LIFE?

_____

_____

_____

_____

Rather than getting stuck in doctrine that doesn't produce fruit, let's look at what is actually taking place. There is clear momentum toward a significant move of the Holy Spirit in our generation. If we see the kingdom of darkness on display, how much more should we anticipate the Kingdom of Light breaking through those clouds with power! Let's take a step back again and take the long view of what has transpired since our Lord's resurrection.

33 AD:	3,000 added at Pentecost
33-100AD (approx.):	Early church enjoys brief period of unity & Kingdom advances
40 – current	Outsiders creep in and dilute the message
200-1500	Very few reports of revivals or significant moves of the Holy Spirit
1450	Printing press invented
1517	Start of Protestant Reformation
1525	First English language Bible translation
1730	First wave of revivals hits with Protestants in US
1730 – current	Five more waves of revival led by Holy Spirit

It's fascinating to look at Christian history from this high up as we ponder why the ways of the Kingdom haven't truly yet advanced through our nations, communities or even churches. Did the lack of Truth/availability of the Bible play a role? It is amazing the printing press, translation of the Bible and reformation all happened in the same era. It's also amazing that revivals have been breaking out since. Looking at the history reminds me of Jesus Words on the clashing of Kingdoms. God in reformation power uniting a body to conquer together.

The kingdom of heaven has been subjected to violence, and violent people have been raiding it. **Matthew 11:12 NIV**

It is now our time of advance, not trying to force our views on others or demand our laws get passed, rather using the blueprint Jesus provided for us. This has started to happen, but only in the last 300 years. There have now been 6 revival periods or "waves" of revival during this period, each with demonstrations of the Kingdom with signs and wonders. There seems to be a Spiritual momentum or "build up" to a massive 7th wave in our generation, which will lead to significant reformation and usher in the greatest harvest of all time. Let's pray and fast together (one day a week?) until we see this manifest! The greatest need of the world today is a mighty manifestation of the Spirit of God in reformation power.

QUESTION:

- WHAT IS THE HOLY SPIRIT SAYING TO ME?

_____

_____

_____

_____

_____

_____

_____

GROUP DISCUSSION:

- WHAT WOULD IT TAKE FOR US TO REMAIN IN UNITY? IT HAS BEEN A FEW WEEKS SINCE WE HAVE PRACTICED THE GIFTS OF THE SPIRIT, HAS ANYONE SENSED THE SPIRIT MOVING AND STEPPED OUT? WHAT HAPPENED?

GROUP ACTIVITY:

- DO A LITTLE MINISTRY TIME TO SEE HOW THE SPIRIT WOULD LIKE TO MOVE AMONG YOU. PRAY TOGETHER AS A GROUP, ASKING THE LORD FOR WORDS AND GUIDANCE FOR WHAT'S NEXT. HOW MANY PEOPLE IN YOUR GROUP WILL COMMIT TO HOSTING ONE OF THESE STUDIES WITH A NEW GROUP? HOW MANY PEOPLE IN THE GROUP HAVE COMMITTED TO ENTERING INTO DISCIPLESHIP RELATIONSHIPS?